The Lost Narrative of Jesus

The Lost Narrative of Jesus

Peter Cresswell

Winchester, UK
Washington, USA

First published by Christian Alternative Books, 2016
Christian Alternative Books is an imprint of John Hunt Publishing Ltd.,
Laurel House, Station Approach,
Alresford, Hants, SO24 9JH, UK
office1@jhpbooks.net
www.johnhuntpublishing.com
www.christian-alternative.com

For distributor details and how to order please visit the 'Ordering' section on our website.

ISBN: 978 1 78535 277 5
Library of Congress Control Number: 2015949730

A CIP catalogue record for this book is available from the British Library.

Design: Stuart Davies

Printed in the USA by Edwards Brothers Malloy

CONTENTS

Acknowledgements

Thanks are due to my wife Julia for her unfailing support and for putting up with yet another 'last book', to my son David and my daughters Fiona and Eloise for their encouragement and technical assistance at various times, to Bill Waghorn for putting me on the trail and exchanging ideas and to Alan Bale for his constructive advice.

Preface

Whether in their original language or in translation, stories have a cultural and historical context. So regard has to be paid to this in their analysis. The text cannot entirely be divorced from the setting in which it was written.

This is as much the case with the stories surrounding Jesus as it is for other characters from past centuries, for which surviving records are also imperfect and often suspect. The task of weighing written record against social reality is made more exacting in this case by the fact that it has largely been appropriated by a religious establishment with its own agenda.

The difficulty in translating from the source texts is here heightened by two factors. The first is that New Testament (koine) Greek is an ancient language. So it is not neither possible to consult with a native speaker nor 'visit' the context, except indirectly, to resolve an issue.

It is sometimes a matter of judgement what usage to choose as an equivalent to the original Greek. It follows that, even for a single source manuscript, there is likely to be no completely authoritative and unchallengeable translation.[1]

The second problem arises from the fact that translations have often been made by linguists who, albeit competent, have a particular set of preconceived beliefs. These can and sometimes do mould and mar their judgment into making a translation that is neither dispassionate nor accurate.[2]

It is my purpose in this book to look at the story of the transfiguration. It appears in the three synoptic gospels, in other non-canonical gospels and in a letter attributed to Peter. It provides a recurrent theme, worked out for the most part in these sources in considerable detail. There are many apparently bizarre and puzzling elements.

When I first looked at the story, I could find no immediate, satisfactory explanations. So, in my earlier consideration of the New Testament, I left it to one side. What finally propelled me to study the transfiguration text was the good advice of a friend. It was, he suggested, something definitely worth looking into.

I had no idea at the outset what the outcome might be. But the conclusion that I did come to, that I have turned over again and again in relation to the evidence, is quite staggering.

The transfiguration story has, I will suggest, been misinterpreted. It has a significance that has thus far been missed. In the course of uncovering its likely meaning and origins I will, at the same time, be able to offer a solution to another great, unresolved, mystery.

There is unfortunately no authoritative framework for the period in which the tale of the transfiguration is set. This creates an immediate problem in carrying out the investigation, as it would for any analysis of similar text: how to relate the study of what is in the story to what was happening at the time, when nothing is agreed.

It would not, I suggest, be appropriate to burden every single exercise in New Testament textual analysis with an original examination of the relevant history which is the period from about CE 30 to 70 for the provinces of Judea and Galilee/Perea. On the other hand, some sense of direction and context is needed and will be relevant.

So what I propose to do is provide some pointers. There is no single source providing definitive answers for the historical background. There is thus also no substitute for doing the reading and research for oneself.

While it may not be what readers are expecting, what I am offering here is not all of the answers, but a task.

Outside of the gospels, there are very few references to the existence of Jesus or a Jesus movement in the first century CE, let alone any details of his life. The most direct occur in the pages of the Jewish historian Josephus and even these are regarded by many scholars as of dubious authenticity. There are passages in a Slavonic version of his earlier work, the *Jewish War,* which may well have originated as later additions. In *Antiquities,* there are two passing references to Jesus that also may be forged or interpolated.

The most compelling evidence from Josephus is not, however, provided by the passages that mention Jesus directly but by a couple of strange and rather gossipy stories in *Antiquities* that have characters in common, and so may be inter-related.[3]

The ostensible purpose of these appears to be to provide explanations or justifications for the persecution, during the reign of the Emperor Tiberius, of priests at the temple of Isis and for the expulsions of Jews from Rome. But the detail suggests another level of interpretation, as parodies firstly of the nativity stories and secondly of Saul's fund-raising activities.

There is, in the latter case, a degree of resonance with accusations of misappropriation levelled against Saul in some sources. And it also fits with Saul's expostulations, in his letters, that he was not, as his opponents were apparently suggesting, misdirecting funds raised for the 'saints' in Jerusalem to his own use.[4]

That Josephus apparently took the trouble to deliver such elaborate put-downs is of itself evidence for the origins and existence of the Jesus movement, though not of course for the veracity of its associated doctrines. No later Christian annotator could, in my view, have generated these scathing asides, perfectly in Josephus' style, as a roundabout way of providing testimony for Christian belief.

The gospels, both canonical and non-canonical, do of course give a lot of details, albeit with some huge gaps, of Jesus' life. Many Christians would argue that this is witness from the immediate followers of Jesus who 'believed' or were converted to a religion generated by Jesus himself.

This is at odds with evidence in Acts and the Letter to the Galatians, attributed to Saul, that the first stage in the creation of

Christianity was a rift within Judaism between more fundamentalist Jews who wanted to adhere, if anything even more zealously, to the Mosaic Laws and others who sought a much a more flexible monotheism, divested of dietary restrictions and the requirement for circumcision (Acts 21, 20-36; Galatians 2, 4; 2 Corinthians 11, 4-6, 12-15; 1 Thessalonians 2, 14-16).

Nor does it fit with evidence in Acts that, following the crucifixion, the followers and family of Jesus continued attending the Temple as observant Jews (Acts 2, 46; 3, 1). Similarly, Saul's sect, while clearly at odds with the movement headed by James, did not immediately take on a non-Jewish identity requiring a new name. It was only later that these breakaway Jews, according to Acts, became known as 'Christians' (Acts 11, 26).

To put it starkly, there were no 'Christians' and no 'Christianity' while Jesus was alive and active, accepting for present purposes that such a character was ever alive and active. Some commentators have indeed argued that Jesus never existed and that this might be the reason that, outside of the gospels, the evidence is so thin.

The Jesus that can be gleaned from all the sources was or would have been a Jew, very much like his brother James. The movement of Nazoreans/Nazarenes within Judaism of which Jesus was a member,[5] and of which Saul was accused of being a member (Acts 24, 5), has strong parallels with that of the authors of the Dead Sea scrolls, as they appear in their own writings and as described by Josephus and others, as Essenes.[6]

James was clearly a figure of great religious authority, who served as a focus of opposition to the collaborating, official Sadducee high priest, imposed on Jews through the Romans. Indeed, it appears that James did actually function as an opposition high priest, entering the 'holy of holies' within the temple on the day of atonement.[7]

The members of the community headed by James were described as, and referred to themselves as, 'the poor', a term that may have related to their practice of sharing property. Probably for the same reason, this was one of the ways in which the authors of some of the Dead Sea scrolls described themselves.

Since it is unlikely that James and Jesus belonged to entirely different groups, the implication is that Nazorean/Nazarene (possibly meaning 'keeper' as in 'keeper of the covenant') was just another label applied to the same broad movement within Judaism in which James and Jesus were both key figures.

So, rather than being a rebel among Jews looking for a new way forward, the Jesus of history may well have been among those who wanted a new covenant, but with even more scrupulous regard to the Jewish Law. If he were also the Jewish king or messiah that Pilate conceded him to be (John 19, 19-22), then he was also seeking a restoration for Jews of political and religious sovereignty.

The character Saul of the gospels (distanced from his evil alter ego, as 'Paul') does have a possible counterpart in the writings of Josephus. This is the Herodian Saul, who persecuted the weak and plundered their property and then sided with the Romans in the Jewish uprising from CE 66-70 (*Antiquities* 20, 9, 4, *Jewish War* 2, 556-558). The relatives to whom Saul sent greetings in one of his letters (Romans 16, 10-11), Aristobulus and Herodion ('little Herod') appear in the Herodian family tree as Saul's closest relatives outside of his own immediate family.[8]

Saul's initial pitch for converts among Jews in the diaspora and in Palestine, as graphically described in Acts and in Saul's letters (Acts 13, 5, 16-45, 50; 14, 19; 1 Thessalonians 2, 14-16), was met with both verbal attacks and physical violence and failed to make real headway. It is surely what would have been expected, given the position taken by the Saul of the New Testament in seeking to subvert Jewish custom and Law. If this character had his roots in the Herodian Saul, then it adds to the plausibility of a likely hostile initial reception among Jews.

While the initial response from Jews was undoubtedly a

major setback, there was still a substantial potential pool of recruits for the new sect from among gentiles (Acts 13, 45-49; 18, 5-6), including both new pagan converts and 'god fearers' prized from Jewish communities in the diaspora and, it would seem, quite a few Herodians from Saul's own circle (Acts 13, 1).

I have suggested[9] that these converts brought with them pre-existing pagan beliefs that would be assimilated into the new Judaism-for-gentiles.

Saul, in the meantime, had been addressing himself in claimed apparitions and dreams (1 Corinthians, 11, 23; 15, 8; Galatians 1, 11-16; Acts 9, 1-9; 22, 6-11; 26, 12-19) to the character Jesus who, according to a Jewish narrative, had recently been crucified and had then reappeared. Thus, Saul could claim to be in touch with a prior authority over James and the other elders/saints in Jerusalem.

The story happened to fit in stunningly well with the pagan myths of his new converts. They could feel comfortable and at home with Jesus as their Dionysus, their dying-and-resurrecting godman. The process of conversion was in this manner eased and gathered momentum.

But Saul was not entirely in control of developments in the scattered communities of followers that he had created, and that could only be reached in person or by letters taking many days or even weeks to arrive.

Saul's letters give evidence of a progression in which Jesus gradually acquired, from pre-existing pagan myth, the quality of being literally, as opposed to metaphorically or in a Jewish sense as a son of David, the son of God.[10] Though Saul was most probably the prime instigator of this new sect, he was not able to determine how its followers responded and he had perforce to adapt.

The Christian view of Jesus starts off with presumptions that are accumulated doctrine, including the 'son of God' idea, brought to the religion by its early converts.

So it is in character theological, rather than historical. The evidence, whatever view one takes, is very largely contained in surviving gospel writings. These show signs of having been edited and adapted over a period to fit with evolving Church doctrine. The narrative provided, in so far as it reflects doctrine, is therefore also theological rather than testimony that can be treated as essentially, though of course imperfectly, historical.

But it is quite likely that the original Christian authors used Jewish sources, written or oral, as well as possibly some Roman records. Indeed, they would have had to, unless inventing the narrative in its entirety, given that these would have been the only sources available. As already pointed out, there were no 'Christians' on the spot to take notes and write up events as these happened. The movement itself that generated such adherents was a product of an interpretation of the events, some years later.

So, were the stories surrounding Jesus, specifically here the transfiguration, simply invented or were they based to some degree on an earlier Jewish narrative? This is one of the questions that can be addressed through textual analysis.[11]

Introduction

The transfiguration story appears in a variety of sources including all three synoptic gospels – Mark, Matthew and Luke – and in some later, non-canonical writings. In the core of the narrative, Jesus and three of his followers go up a high mountain. Jesus' garments glisten, intensely white.

The long-dead figures of Moses and Elijah appear and talk with Jesus.

A cloud overshadows them. Then a voice, it can be presumed of God, from the cloud declares Jesus to be his 'son, the beloved'. The voice commands the three companions to listen to Jesus.

This sequence, as it now reads, appears to have a central purpose. This is to give Jesus precedence over two figures, identified as Moses and Elijah, who represent Jewish Law and the prophets. Moreover, Jesus' standing is on the highest authority. It is God-given.

Placed as it is within the gospels and framed as it is, it is clearly a Christian construction.

There are, however, a number of discordant and often very puzzling elements in the story as a whole that deserve investigation and hopefully can be afforded an explanation.

The transfiguration narrative is very similar in each of the synoptic gospels though there are differences, some of which subsequent analysis will show to be significant. The parallels between the different versions derive from the fact that these gospels rely substantially on a common body of source material.

Mark was, on the evidence, the first of the gospels to be written and used as a source by the authors of Matthew and Luke.[1] Though it was probably initially compiled around CE 80, there are no surviving manuscripts from this period for Mark, or indeed for any of the other gospels.

For Mark's account, we rely largely on codices from the mid-fourth century, though there is a surviving papyrus manuscript (**P45**) from the third century that has part of the transfiguration narrative, while missing nearly all of the passion sequence.

The author of Matthew copied large sections of Mark almost verbatim and there are passages in Luke that were clearly also taken from Mark.

It seems likely that the authors of Matthew and Luke used an archetype gospel of Mark, as opposed to the original source or sources used by the author of Mark.

This would, for example, explain why these gospels lack any convincing ending following the discovery, after the crucifixion, of an empty tomb. Most scholars acknowledge that the last twelve verses of Mark present in some manuscripts constitute a later, possibly second-century, addition to make up for what appeared as an unsatisfactory conclusion. The authors of Matthew and Luke cease to follow the longer version of Mark at this point because what they used as their source was the version of Mark ending at verse 16, 8.

This archetype of Mark, used by the later gospel writers, was not necessarily an original version. It might already have been changed several times during its composition. And there is also the possibility that it represented, in its initial form, a rewriting of either a Jewish story or a Jewish portrayal of events.

Some elements, unique to Luke, indicate that the writer of this gospel may also have had access to an early variation of Mark (also ending at verse 16, 8) or possibly another version of the passion narrative, other traces of which have since been lost.

There are certainly aspects of the transfiguration narrative that, at first glance, simply do not make sense or do not fit well into the context of the story as a whole or appear unduly strained.

There are some guidelines that can be taken in analysing a text that may have been in its inception a rewritten account. In the first place, an earlier Jewish storyteller's agenda would likely have been quite different from that of a later Christian editor or adaptor. As already noted, the generation of Saul's sect was marked by schism and a struggle over the retention or rejection of some Jewish laws, customary practices and values. So some rewriting, not necessarily of history but at least of the storyline, is to be expected in the Christian account.

If there are elements that conflict with the Christian perspective that is being projected, then there is a good chance that these will be more original. This is because a Christian author would hardly have introduced something at odds with the message that he wished to promote.

It is also not so likely that the discordant notes could have arisen accidentally and then been overlooked. A more plausible scenario arises from the fact that one change often necessitates further changes in characters and circumstances at other points in a story to make everything still fit. Inevitably, when there is such editing, one or two of these details will be left in their more original form, providing witness of an earlier version. The text will need to be examined to see if there is any evidence of this.

If inconsistent, implausible or apparently nonsensical elements are to be attributed to such factors as accidental errors in copying, mistranslation or simply a storyteller's incompetence, then it might be expected that taken together these will form no obvious pattern. If, on the other hand, a number of such elements do fit together with each other, then it suggests that they were part of a more original story that has been written over and adapted.

If the pattern so formed makes sense as part of the structure of an alternative narrative, then this will reinforce the case that what the text is indicating is an imperfect effort to transform and supplant that narrative.

Any alternative narrative so deduced can then be reapplied to the whole of the text to see whether the drift of details support this or the agenda that has been found to be superimposed.

It is possible that Christian writers will, in many instances, have simply used the material that they had to hand and in so doing have made something a little different, or more suited to their purposes. But, in other cases, there may have been a definite motivation to counter and supplant an original that conflicted with the writer's new agenda. Such directed editing can be found in many other gospel stories.[2] It would not therefore be unexpected to find it present in this case also.

The transfiguration account does not exist in the gospels and in other texts in isolation. The language used and the construction of the story can be examined to see how these compare with other parts of the same text and with other texts from the same, or from earlier periods.

Some of these lines of investigation may provide an answer as to why and how the story was included in Mark, the first of the surviving gospels.

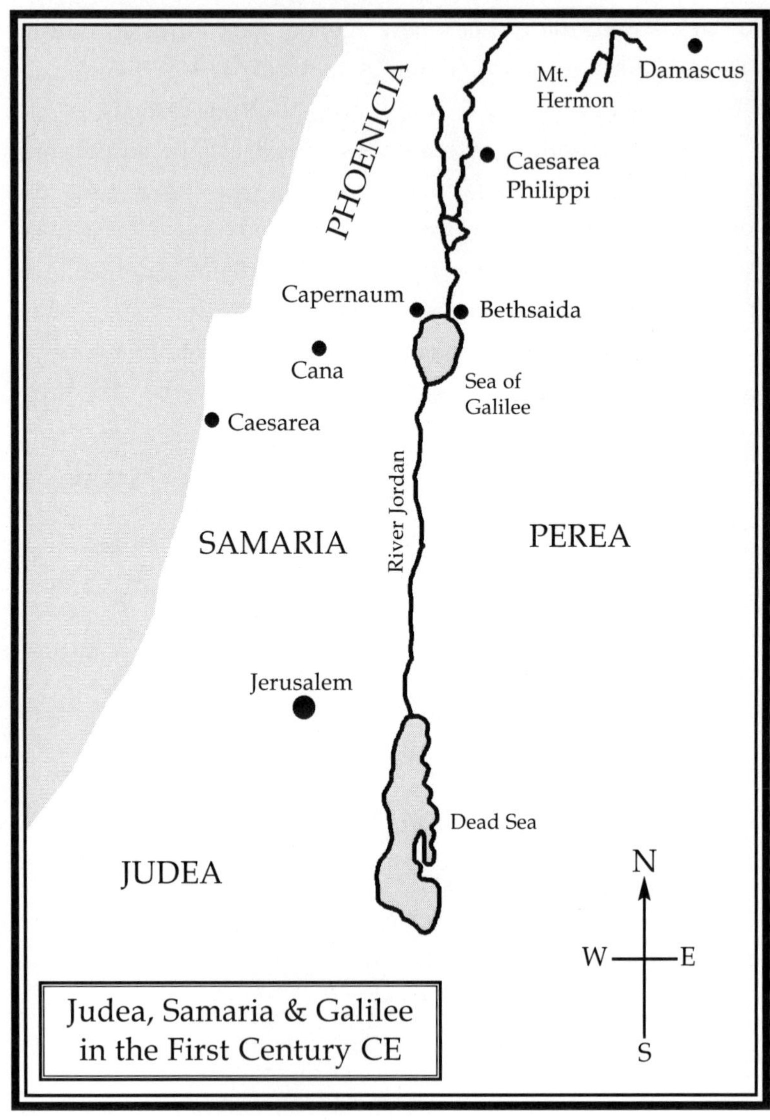

Judea, Samaria & Galilee in the First Century CE

Chapter One

According to Mark

And Jesus went on with his disciples to the villages of Caesarea Philippi.

And on the way he asked his disciples, 'Who do people say I am?' And they replied to him, 'John the Baptist, and others Elijah, and still others one of the prophets.'

He asked them, 'But who do you say that I am?'

Peter replied, 'You are the messiah.' And he warned them that they should not tell anyone about him.

Then he began to teach them that son of man must undergo great suffering and be rejected by the elders, the chief priests and the scribes and be killed and after three days rise again.

He said all this quite openly. And Peter took him aside and began to rebuke him. But, turning around and looking at his disciples, he rebuked Peter, saying, 'Get behind me, Satan! For, you are not considering the things of God but the things of men.'

He called the crowd with his disciples, and said to them, 'If anyone wants to become my follower, let him deny himself, take up his cross and follow me. For whoever seeks to save his life will lose it, and whoever loses his life for my sake and for the sake of the gospel will save it. For what does it benefit a man to gain the whole world but forfeits his life? Indeed, what can a man be given in return for his life?

For whoever is ashamed of me and my words, in this adulterous and sinful generation, of him the son of man will also be ashamed when he comes in the glory of his father with the holy angels'.

And he said to them, 'Truly I tell you there are some standing here who will not taste death until they have seen that the kingdom of God has come with power.'

And after six days, Jesus took Peter, James and John and led them up a high mountain, privately by themselves.

And he was transfigured before them and his clothes became a dazzling white, such that no fuller on earth could bleach them. And there appeared to them Elijah with Moses, who were talking with Jesus.

Then Peter said to Jesus, 'Rabbi, it is good for us to be here, so let us make three tents [CKHNAC], one for you and one for Moses and one for Elijah.' He had not known what he was saying (or 'what to say'), for they were terrified.

Then a cloud overshadowed them and out of the cloud there came a voice, 'This is my son, the beloved; listen to him.' And suddenly, when they looked around, they no longer saw anyone except Jesus alone with them.

And, as they were coming down from the mountain, he ordered them to tell no one what they had seen, until after the son of man had risen from the dead. So they kept the matter to themselves, questioning what 'rising from the dead' could mean.

And they asked him, 'Why do the scribes say that Elijah must come first?'

And he said to them, 'Elijah indeed comes first to restore all things.'

And how was it written concerning the son of man that he must suffer many things and be rejected?

But I tell you that Elijah has come and they did to him whatever they pleased, just as it was written concerning him.

When they came to the disciples, they saw a great crowd around them and some scribes arguing with them. When the whole crowd saw him, they were immediately amazed and ran forward to greet him.

And he questioned them, 'What are you arguing about with them [the scribes]?'

And someone from the crowd answered him, 'Teacher, I brought you my son; he has a spirit that makes him unable to speak and, whenever it seizes him, it throws him down and he foams at the mouth and grinds his teeth and becomes rigid, and I asked your disciples to cast it out but they could not do it.'

Mark 8, 27 – 9, 18

The extract given above comes from the critical text, which is dependent on the fourth-century parchment codices, Codex Sinaiticus and Codex Vaticanus. But the story itself may have been first formulated in the late first century.

I have divided up the text to highlight the framework of the narrative and excursions into acts of healings, sayings and commentary, attributed to Jesus, attached to it. It was recognised that the early gospel writers did not have any exact chronology for the events they recorded or for remembered sayings and conversations. So the placing of these, whether or not accurate in themselves, is not always going to be reliable.

It has been suggested that the synoptic gospel authors, as well as working from one or more passion narratives, also used a hypothesised collection of sayings (sayings gospel Q) that they then wove into the text.

The warning to the disciples of Jesus' imminent suffering and death, in the above extract, follows a standard formula. It is, I suggest, a Christian take, intended to show that Jesus (being part God) was in control of his destiny as opposed to being a victim of circumstance. Jesus is also, on the journey from Bethsaida to villages in the region of Caesarea Philippi, given to address a crowd on the benefits of following him and to extract from his key disciple Peter an admission that he was the messiah.

That this is also an artifice can be seen from that fact that, if Jesus had claims to the throne of David (and it appeared from his actions and from Pilate's responses that he had) then his close followers and family would all along have known on what grounds – specifically the line of descent – this was based.

Peter could not, in a first-century context and while Jesus was alive, have understood him to be a Christian messiah, in terms of a framework of ideas that was yet to be created.

The speculation as to Jesus' role or identity, attributed to a wider audience, repeats material used earlier in Mark. In the story describing the death of John the Baptist, Herod learns that people have been saying that the healer Jesus was either John, raised from the dead, or Elijah reincarnated or a prophet, like one of the prophets of old (Mark 6, 15).

Jesus goes on with Peter, James and John to reach what is described as a 'high mountain'. Given this reference and the direction of travel from Bethsaida by the Sea of Galilee towards the villages of Caesarea Philippi, there is a strong presumption that the destination intended was Mount Hermon, which was certainly high at over 9,000 feet.

The story begins with a reference to the time, six days, that it had taken to get to the mountain. After the transfiguration event, the narrative continues with an account of what happened on the way before merging, not at all seamlessly, at the end into a typical healing miracle story.

The main elements of the transfiguration, as it can be seen, do serve a specific purpose. The long-dead and possibly even mythical Jewish figures of Moses and Elijah are summoned to appear before Jesus and three of his disciples. The disciples witness the voice of God, speaking from a cloud, pronouncing Jesus as his son and, at the same time giving him precedence over the figurehead representatives of the Jewish Law and prophets, Moses and Elijah.

The message is clear. The old order is over, or at least has reached its fulfilment in Jesus. God's religion is no longer the Judaism of the Old Testament, but Christianity.

There are a number of more minor details that could fit with this as a Christian-invented story. Mountains were often seen as sacred, so this would have been an appropriate location for God to deliver a message, just as in the Old Testament story of Moses and the ten commandments.

The meeting was conducted in secret. After the event, the disciples were sworn to secrecy, as they were also on the way to the mountain in respect of Jesus' messianic identity. The purpose, it has to be presumed at this point, would have been to avoid

Jesus being pre-emptively caught and executed. This would have been, according to Christian doctrine, so that he could achieve precisely the same outcome at a subsequent time of his choosing.

Of course, if the disciples kept their vow, the story would logically never have come to light and been written down. The editor/storyteller gets round this by qualifying the command to silence until 'after the son of man had risen from the dead'.

It has also to be supposed that the disciples did not understand this.

This is more than a little clumsy.[1] The text has been fashioned to convey a Christian explanation, incomprehensible in its historical context, that Jesus was intent on fulfilling a cosmic purpose. The commonsense explanation is that, as a prominent Nazorean leader, Jesus would have wanted to help oust the Romans while avoiding being crucified (though ultimately failing in both respects).

In order to sustain the fiction, the disciples are made to appear as dumb and uncomprehending, unaware of a greater, divine purpose. In the context, they were of course unaware of any such agenda, as Jewish followers of a Jewish messiah. They would certainly have been aware of Jesus' credentials and, like other Jews, would have had no problem understanding 'what rising from the dead could mean'.

The gloss is there to explain away what would at the time have appeared as an awkward fact. Not only were the family and followers of Jesus not Christians, but they were in the first century involved in conflict with the Jewish breakaway sect's first followers.

It is not easy to find an immediate explanation for some of the elements of the narrative. One curious feature is the proposed provision of tents for the ghostly visitors. Such equipment could not have been found at the top of a high mountain. But the story does not explain why the disciples might have taken tents with them.

The precedent for Jesus' metamorphosis is presumably the story of Moses, whose face shone after encountering God on Mount Sinai (Exodus 34, 29-35). However, there is no direct reference here to any visual transformation. It is, rather, Jesus' clothes that shine.

Before embarking on further analysis, there are two other synoptic accounts of the transfiguration, as well as some other versions, that need to be considered. I will therefore look next at the stories of the transfiguration in the gospels of Matthew and Luke.

It may be that these, though later in origin than Mark and to a great extent dependent on Mark as their source, will cast more light on the situation.

As prelude to this, I draw attention to a major anomaly, which the reader may already have noticed, by pointing to a fact of geography.

The text from Mark 8, 27 to 9, 1 describes a journey from Bethsaida by the Sea of Galilee to Caesarea Philippi and what was said on the way. The route would have involved a relatively gentle ascent along a valley, beside streams making up the river Jordan. The total distance was about 24 miles over not too difficult terrain. At a time when walking was the major form of transport for most people, and for men used to hard physical labour and an outdoor way of life, this journey could have been achieved in a day.

So why does the author of Mark introduce an unexplained gap of six days? This could not simply have been the time taken to undertake such a relatively short journey. So is he pointing to something else that happened in the time frame, but failing to describe it? Or is the reference to six days an error or an intrusion from some other part of the narrative?

There is something amiss here with the text. Just what, I hope to find out.

Chapter Two

According to Matthew and Luke

Now, when Jesus came into the region of Caesarea Philippi, he asked his disciples, 'Who do people say is the son of man?' and they said, 'Some say John the Baptist, but others Elijah and still others Jeremiah or one of the prophets.'

He said to them, 'But who do you consider me to be?'

And Simon Peter replied, 'You are the messiah, the son of the living God.'

And Jesus answered him, 'Blessed are you Simon Bariona [the Outlaw]. For flesh and blood has not revealed this to you, but my father in heaven.'

'And I tell you, you are Peter [ΠЄΤΡΟC rock] and on this rock I will build my church and the gates of Hades will not prevail against it.'

'I will give you the keys of the kingdom of heaven, and whatever you bind on earth will be bound in heaven and whatever you loose on earth will be loosed in heaven.'

Then he ordered the disciples not to tell anyone that he was the messiah.

From that time on, Jesus began to explain to his disciples that he had to go to Jerusalem and undergo great suffering at the hands of the elders and chief priests and scribes and be killed and on the third day be raised.

And Peter took him aside and began to rebuke him, saying, 'May God be gracious to you, Lord, that this will never happen to you.'

But he turned around and said to Peter, 'Get behind me, Satan! You are a stumbling block to me; you are not considering the things of God, but the things of men.'

Then Jesus said to his disciples, 'If anyone wants to be my follower, let him deny himself, take up his cross and follow me. For whoever seeks to save his life will lose it, and whoever loses his life for my sake will find it. For what does it benefit a man, if he gains the whole world but forfeits his life? Or what can a man be given in exchange for his life? For the son of man will come in the glory of his father and with his angels and then he will repay everyone according to their actions. Truly I tell you there are some standing here who will not taste death until they have seen the son of man coming in his kingdom.'

And after six days, Jesus took Peter and James and his brother John and led them up a high mountain privately.

And he was transfigured before them and his face shone like the sun and his clothes became as white as the light. Suddenly, there appeared to them Moses and Elijah, talking with him.

Then Peter said to Jesus, 'Lord, it is good for us to be here. If you wish, I will make three tents [CKHNAC] here, one for you and one for Moses and one for Elijah.'

While he was speaking, suddenly a bright cloud overshadowed them and out of the cloud a voice said, 'This is my son, the beloved, with whom I am well pleased; listen to him.'

When the disciples heard this, they fell on their faces and were overcome with fear. But Jesus came and touched them and said, 'Get up and do not be afraid'. And when they looked up, they saw no one except Jesus alone.

And, as they were coming down from the mountain, Jesus ordered them, 'Tell no one about the vision until the son of man has been raised from the dead.'

And the disciples asked him, 'Why then do the scribes say that Elijah must come first?'

And he replied, 'Elijah indeed is coming and will restore all things. But I tell you that Elijah has already come and they did not recognise him but did to him whatever they wished. So also is the son of man about to suffer at their hands.' Then the disciples understood that he was speaking to them about John the Baptist.

When they came to the crowd, a man came to him, knelt before him and said, 'Lord have mercy on my son for he is an epileptic …'

Matthew 16, 13 – 17, 14

It happened that, while Jesus was praying alone with only the disciples near him, he asked them, 'Who do the crowds say that I am?'

They answered, 'John the Baptist, and others Elijah, and still others that one of the ancient prophets has risen.'

He said to them, 'But who do you say than I am?'

Peter answered, 'The messiah of God'.

He warned them and ordered them not to tell anyone.

Then he said that the son of man must suffer much and be rejected by the elders and the chief priests and the scribes and be killed and on the third day be raised.

Then he said, 'If anyone wishes to follow me, let him deny himself and take up his cross daily and follow me. For whoever wishes to save his life will lose it. But whoever loses his life on account of me will save it. For what does it profit a man, if he gains the world but loses or forfeits himself?'

'For whoever is ashamed of me and my words, of him the son of man will be ashamed when he comes in his glory and the glory of the father and the holy angels. But truly I tell you there are some standing here who will not taste death before they see the kingdom of God.'

Now about eight days after these sayings, Jesus took Peter and John and James and went up on the mountain to pray.

And while he prayed, the appearance of his face changed and his clothes became dazzling white. Suddenly, two men were talking with him, who were Moses and Elijah. They appeared in glory and were speaking of his departure [EXOΔON] which he was about to accomplish in Jerusalem. Now Peter and his companions had been weighed down with sleep, but having awakened fully (or 'stayed awake'), they saw his glory and the two men who stood with him.

As they were leaving him, Peter said to Jesus, 'Master, it is good for us to be here; so let us make three tents [CKHNAC], one for you and one for Moses and one for Elijah.' – not knowing what he said.

And, while he was saying this, a cloud came and overshadowed them and they were afraid as they entered the cloud. Then, from the cloud came a voice that said, 'This is my son, the chosen one; listen to him.' When the voice had spoken, Jesus was found alone. And they kept silent, and in those days told no one any of things they had seen.

On the following day, when they had come down from the mountain, a great crowd met him. Just then, a man from the crowd shouted, 'Teacher, I beg you to look at my son, my only child ... '

Luke 9, 18-38

The examination of these other versions of the transfiguration story brings out some interesting conclusions.

It can be seen, in the first place, how closely the authors of Matthew and Luke have followed Mark's text. In many places, the wording is either very nearly or exactly the same. Essentially, the same framework is adopted in all three cases:

Jesus is on his way from Bethsaida in Galilee to villages in the region of the town of Caesarea Philippi. On the way, he questions the disciples as to how people perceive his identity. He calls people to follow him.

Jesus takes Peter, James and John up a high mountain where the 'transfiguration' event occurs. These disciples are sworn to secrecy.

When they get down the mountain, they encounter his other disciples together with a large crowd of people. Jesus conducts an act of healing which these disciples had failed to achieve.

Matthew elaborates on the text in a number of ways. He is the only writer to include a commission given to Peter by Jesus to found a church, something that also can be read as giving Peter power, as Jesus' prime commander or minister, to make decisions. This is quite likely to have been an addition to the text made some time after this gospel was first written (1).

The passage in which the disciples fall prostrate, after God has spoken, echoes in language and construction Daniel's vision of a heavenly being (Daniel 10, 4-12).

To Mark's version of God's speech from the cloud, the author of Matthew adds, 'with whom I am well pleased', so that it precisely matches the words attributed to God earlier in Matthew at Jesus' baptism.

The author deletes, after the report that Jesus' clothes became dazzling white, the elaboration, 'such that no fuller on earth could bleach them' and the additional information that the crowd who came to greet Jesus, on coming down from the mountain, were 'amazed'.

He substitutes the Christian term 'Lord' for the Jewish term, 'rabbi', when Peter addresses Jesus. Luke similarly substitutes 'master' for 'rabbi'.

Jews at the time, and this would most certainly have included Jesus' followers, believed in 'No Lord but God' and fought for their freedom from the Romans under this slogan. Thus, in these ways, the usages in Matthew and Luke represent a further progression in the Christian reworking of the text.

Matthew reworks Jesus' response to a question on the expected return of Elijah, adding some details and deleting others. As will be seen, these changes are significant. He comments that the disciples understood Jesus as saying that 'he was speaking to them about John the Baptist'.

He amends Peter's response on seeing Moses and Elijah, removing the implication that Peter was struggling with what to say, and possibly confused, in offering the two ethereal visitors the hospitality of what would have been the disciples' own tents in which to sleep. This is, however, an element that the author of Luke, retains.

While Luke also eliminates the note that the crowd were amazed to see Jesus and ran forward, when the four of them came down from the mountain, he adds – or gives – a further piece of interesting information. He tells us what the men on the mountain and Jesus were talking about, or at least one of the things they were talking about. The subject of their conversation was most surprisingly, in the context, Jesus' forthcoming exile [EXOΔON] in Jerusalem.

Luke also uniquely provides another piece of information. This is that Peter and the others are described as being 'weighed down with sleep' before seeing and hearing Jesus talking with two men. They were either tired, having just climbed the mountain, or it was late in the day, or possibly both. Only Luke indicates that they may well have spent the night on the mountain, describing Jesus and his companions as encountering the waiting crowd 'on the following day'.

Luke's additional detail, including the subject of conversation on the mountain, indicates that the author might have had an additional source beside Mark's text. On the other hand, both Luke and Matthew clearly did use Mark, following the text for the most part while eliminating or changing some details. It could be that a version of Mark, available at around the end of the first century to the authors of these later gospels, did have more detail.

On this interpretation, Luke has used information that was in Mark then, but has subsequently been eliminated.

For Matthew we are, as with Mark, primarily dependent on the fourth-century sources, though there is part of the transfiguration narrative for Mark in the earlier papyrus source from the third century, **P**45. For Luke, we have both **P**45 and another even earlier manuscript, possibly from as early as the late second century, **P**75.

This is helpful in that it indicates that the present form of the narrative was generated early on, since Luke in these very early papyrus sources follows the text of Mark.

However, as I have argued, it does seem that in some respects the source that the author of Luke was using was a version of Mark that was a work in progress.

Matthew and Mark offer a similar treatment of the men with whom Jesus is described as talking. There are two references in each to Moses and Elijah.

In Luke, however, there are not two but three references to the men that Jesus, Peter, John and James are described as having met. In the second reference they are described as just 'two men'. In the first, Jesus' supporters suddenly see 'two men who were conversing with him', a subtly different nuance from them suddenly appearing, as in Mark and Matthew. This reference has an awkward qualification, 'who were Moses and Elijah', which may well at some point have been incorporated from a marginal note.

It is only in the third reference, 'just as they were leaving him', when it no longer makes sense, is there Peter's full-blown statement, 'Master, it is good for us to be here; so let us make three tents, one for you, one for Moses and one for Elijah.'

Luke's text shows signs of having been edited to create a version, in which Jesus meets up with Moses and Elijah, from one in which he simply encountered two men, nameless in the story but possibly identified in an even earlier source. It has apparently been harmonised with the text that is now in Mark and Matthew.

This in turn suggests that the author of Luke may have been using a version of Mark that not only predates what now appears in Mark, but also possibly the version that the author of Matthew was using.

The discrepancies and oddities in these three accounts are beginning to mount up, and becoming harder to explain.

At the end of the previous chapter, I drew attention to the fact that it should not have taken anything like six days, or even 'about eight days' in Luke's version, to get from Bethsaida to Caesarea Philippi (only about 24 miles away). So, why is this time gap so pointedly introduced? Was it to allow for other things happening in the time frame? Or does it rather show that that a greater distance had in fact been travelled to reach Caesarea Philippi?

And what about this meeting, held in great secrecy? It seems that all the other disciples were in the vicinity and knew about it.

There was also a large crowd at the foot of the mountain waiting to see Jesus. So these people had discovered or had been informed that Jesus was going to be there.

What, it must also be wondered, were the scribes doing on the scene? Were they drawn by the disciples, the crowd or the expected presence of Jesus? Did they have an inkling of what was going on?

Why, moreover, were the crowd so amazed just to see Jesus that people ran forward in their efforts to get to him? He was simply coming down from a mountain. He was not, as it appears from the text, performing any miracle at the time. It was also a 'great' crowd. Why were so many gathered at that particular time?

Why before Jesus' mission (however formulated) was accomplished, was he apparently contemplating, like a modern-day pope, the option of retirement or exile (EXOΔON)?

To take some smaller details, why did the three disciples take tents with them up the mountain?

While this detail might appear startlingly modern, there had even then been a very long period in the development and refinement of the art of tent making. Portable tents made from animal hide or wool would have been both practical and effective. But why were they needed either for Jesus and his disciples or for their two guests?

Why did these particular disciples – John, James and Peter – go with Jesus and not some of the others? Would it have mattered which disciples took part in this mission?

And why a meeting on a mountain? Surely, it would have been a most inconvenient place. If there were two other men there (by some arrangement), who were there, how did they get there and where did they come from?

What, crucially, were the scribes and the disciples who stayed behind arguing about? The topic of the dispute is omitted in Mark, leaving the text to run awkwardly into another, quite possibly unrelated, story. Then, even the fact of the dispute itself is excised in the subsequent gospels of Matthew and Luke.

Where does the concern about Elijah 'coming first' fit into the story? Was this just an academic discussion of Jewish eschatology, which happened to be conducted, possibly, as Jesus and his disciples were coming down the mountain? Or did it have some more specific and relevant bearing on the story?

I hope to engage successfully with these questions in the course of my exploration of the transfiguration texts.

The synoptic gospel writers were, however, not the only ones at an early time to take a strong interest in the transfiguration story. Other varieties of Christian, who would have been and were regarded as heretical by the mainstream, docetists and gnostics, also had their versions.

It was certainly an imaginative, dramatic and compelling tale. That is one reason why so many others, among the accounts that still survive, have subsequently taken it up.

The story, with its spiritual and transformational elements, did also provide a useful framework on which to hang the new interpretations of the nature of Jesus, which were being developed from the second century onwards.

Chapter Three

According to Peter, Andrew and John

And the Lord said, 'Let us go to the mountain and pray.' And, going with him, we the twelve disciples besought him that he would show us one of our righteous brethren that had departed out of the world, that we might see what manner of men they are in their form, and take courage, and encourage also the men that should hear us.

And, as we prayed, suddenly there appeared two men standing before the Lord towards the East, upon whom we were not able to look. For there issued from their countenance a ray as of the sun, and their clothing was shining so as the eye of man never saw the like: for no mouth is able to declare nor heart to conceive the glory wherewith they were clad and the beauty of their countenance. When we saw them we were astonished, for their bodies were whiter than any snow and redder than any rose. And the redness of them was mingled with the whiteness, and, in a word, I am not able to declare their beauty. For their hair was curling and flourishing, and fell comely about their countenance and their shoulders like a garland woven of nard and various flowers, or like a rainbow in the air: such was their comeliness.

We, then, seeing their beauty, were astonished at them, for they appeared suddenly. And I drew near to the Lord and said, 'Who are these?'

He said to me, 'These are your righteous brethren whose appearance you did desire to see.'

Apocalypse of Peter 4-13, 2nd century, Akhmim fragment, possibly part of the Gospel of Peter, from translation by M R James

And at another time he took with him James and Peter and I to the mountain where he was accustomed to pray, and we saw in him a light such that it is not possible for a man who uses mortal speech to describe what it was like. Again, in like manner, he brought us three up into the mountain, saying, 'Come ye with me.' So we went again and we saw him at a distance praying. I, therefore, because he loved me, drew nigh to him softly, as though he could not see me, and stood looking at him from behind. And I saw that he was not in any wise clad with garments, but was seen of us naked, and not in any wise as a man, and that his feet were whiter than any snow, so that the earth there was lighted up by his feet, and that his head touched the heaven, so that I was afraid and cried out. And he, turning about, appeared as a man of small stature, and caught hold of my beard and pulled it and said to me, 'John, be not faithless but believing, and not curious.' And I said unto him, 'But what have I done, Lord?' And I say unto you, brethren, I suffered so great pain in that place where he took hold on my beard for thirty days, that I said to him, 'Lord, if your twitch when you were in sport has given me such great pain, what would it be like if you had given me a buffet?' And he said to me, 'Let it be yours henceforth not to tempt him that cannot be tempted.'

But Peter and James were angry because I spoke with the Lord, and beckoned to me that I should come to them and leave the Lord alone. And I went, and they both said to me, 'He [the old man] who was speaking with the Lord on the top of the mount, who was he? For we heard both of them speaking.' And I, having in mind his great grace, and his unity which has many faces, and his wisdom that without ceasing looks upon us, said, 'That you shall learn if you ask him.'

Acts of John, 90-91, late 2nd century, translated by M R James

On the next night he saw a vision which he related.

'Listen, beloved, to my vision. I beheld, and lo, a great mountain raised up on high, which had on it nothing earthly, but only shone with such light, that it seemed to enlighten all the world. And lo, there stood by me my beloved brethren the apostles Peter and John; and John reached his hand to Peter and raised him to the top of the mount, and turned to me and asked me to go up after Peter, saying, 'Andrew, you are to drink Peter's cup.'

And he stretched out his hands and said. 'Draw near to me and stretch out your hands so as to join them to mine, and put your head by my head.' When I did so I found myself shorter than John. After that he said to me, 'Do you wish to know the image of that which you see, and who it is that speaks to you?' And I said, 'I desire to know it.' And he said to me, 'I am the word of the cross whereon you shall hang shortly, for his name's sake whom you preach. And he said to me many other things, of which I must now say nothing, but they shall be declared when I come unto the sacrifice.

Acts of Andrew, 20, 3rd century, from abstract by Gregory, Bishop of Tours, 6th century CE, translated by M R James

These versions of the transfiguration, attributed to Peter, Andrew and John, demonstrate how the Christian texts were beginning to diversify at an early stage. Two of them may well be as old, in origin, as the gospel of Luke. Though having some decidedly weird elements, they are therefore not lightly to be disregarded.

The Apocalypse of Peter, which some scholars believe may have been part of the Gospel of Peter, treats the men that Jesus and his followers meet as spiritual beings as opposed to ordinary mortal men, just like the synoptic gospels. But the agenda behind the inclusion of Moses and Elijah, the twin representatives of Jewish Law and the prophets, has been disregarded. Or, quite possibly, the writer was not even aware of it.

Though by no means conclusive as evidence, this is consistent with the theory that Jesus and his three companions may, in an original Jewish story, have simply met with some other people on the mountain, with the explanation that these were Moses and Elijah introduced later.

What is common to the Apocalypse of Peter version and to the synoptic gospels, and thus has to be explained or explained away, is the 'two men' that (just as in Luke) Jesus and his three followers meet. They are here depicted as some of the righteous departed, conjured up by Jesus for his disciples to see, in all their awesome glory.

Both the Greek Akhmim fragment and an Ethiopic version of the same text, or at least the same story, have Jesus showing his followers visions of heaven, where the righteous will go or have gone, and of a place of punishment for the wicked.

It has been claimed that the content of the Apocalypse of Peter supports the argument that the transfiguration is a post-resurrection tale, on the basis that it is followed by visitations to heaven and hell. What are being described, however, are not visits but visions presented to the disciples, which could (both arguably as an actual event and in the course of a story) have occurred in Jesus' lifetime.

I will in any case subsequently be arguing that the post-resurrection thesis is misguided (see pp 37, 137-139).

In the Acts of John, Jesus appears as a shape-shifter, a common gnostic theme. At one point, he is so tall that his head touches the heavens (echoing the narrative in the gospel of Peter, as Jesus is helped from the tomb). Then, he is smaller than the narrator. He is observed talking to an old man whom, it is apparent from the concluding commentary, is simply another manifestation of Jesus himself. Thus, in this version, the men whom the disciples meet have been made to disappear. Jesus is talking to himself.

The Acts of Andrew, as summarised by Bishop Gregory, offers yet another angle. There is some more shape shifting; John is there to represent the cross on which Andrew is to hang. Like his brother Peter, in the Acts of Peter, his fate is being foreshadowed.

But there is no Jesus present in this story. The two men, here witnessed by Andrew, have become two other disciples, Peter and John.

The transfiguration makes for a compelling tale, with a number of dramatic elements: a meeting held in secrecy, a high and sacred mountain, mysterious strangers, heavenly light, the voice of God. So that is one reason it was taken up and elaborated, to sometimes different ends, by various early Christian groups. It well may be that there were other versions circulating about the same time that have not survived.

The story can also be taken to define Jesus or his role or that of key disciples, as in the Acts of Andrew. It was thus a useful building block for any Christian account.

But alternative presentations such as these may also have been puzzling and possibly threatening to a Christian understanding of Jesus.

What shows through in these, as in the gospel versions, is a meeting commonly known to have taken place between Jesus together with some of his followers and two men, in secret and in an inaccessible place. If the theological accretions are stripped away, there is nothing in the Christian narrative that explains how and why this meeting took place and why it was held under such conditions.

This suggests that the explanation may have lain elsewhere. There is, or rather was, another version, a Jewish story that made sense, which Christians of all kinds had to counter.

These later versions of the transfiguration are certainly interesting and worthy of studying in their own right. For my present purpose, however, I propose to examine in more detail the version that appears in Mark, and has been copied to a great extent in both Matthew and Luke.

Mark is believed to have been first compiled in the latter part of the first century, though the earliest surviving manuscript of the gospel, **P45,** is from the early third century.

This fragmentary papyrus scroll contains part of the transfiguration sequence. This lends weight to the case that it was also there in some form in Mark's first version.

Chapter Four

Examining the Text

An examination of the text needs to begin with the Mark, since the other synoptic gospels of Matthew and Luke are dependent on it. Both these gospels have long stretches that replicate Mark, in considerable detail, sometimes to the point of following the narrative word for word. There are some important variations, especially in Luke, that will also need to be considered.

I will pick out crucial indicators that, I suggest, point in the same direction and examine the whole text to see how minor and circumstantial detail, much of it otherwise quite puzzling, fits in with the picture that emerges.

'Six days later'

What is of prime significance for Mark's more original version is that the whole transfiguration sequence shows signs of having been displaced from somewhere else. There are major dislocations at the beginning (9, 2) and at the end (9, 16) with the preceding and succeeding text.

The story begins abruptly with the phrase 'six days later', with no inkling of why there has been this passage of time and what might be its significance. It would appear that Jesus and his disciples have travelled from Bethsaida (8, 22) towards Caesarea Philippi (8, 27) from which point, after a gap of six days, Jesus took three of his disciples up a high mountain.

Since the journey as described to the vicinity of Caesarea Philippi was only about 24 miles, the time lag makes no sense, unless the transfiguration story were originally placed in another context.

At the end of the transfiguration passage, Jesus is given to ask his disciples what they were arguing about with some scribes.

But the question is not answered. Instead, someone from the crowd replies to something Jesus has apparently said to them but is not at this point recorded. It can be seen then that this ensuing text does not flow from what has gone before. Dislocations such as these are often found to be markers of points where one piece of text has been added to another, sometimes from a separate source. In this case, there are two such breaks that mark the beginning and end of a discrete piece of text dealing with a specific topic: Jesus and his companions on a high mountain. This indicates quite strongly that the whole of this piece of text originated from somewhere else.

Indeed, the link between the text that precedes and succeeds it reinforces the case. The text flows quite smoothly, if the whole of the transfiguration passage from 9, 2 to 9, 16 is taken as an interpolation and left out:

People are bringing sick people to Jesus to be healed, first at Bethsaida (8, 22). Then, somewhere among the villages of Caesarea Philippi, Jesus calls a crowd who were there with his disciples (8, 34). The disciples are mentioned here because this sets the stage: they are going to be identified as having failed in an exercise of healing.

Jesus then addresses the crowd. And someone from the crowd responds, with verse 9, 17 following on from 9, 1, requesting Jesus to heal his child, after the disciples have been unable to do this:

> 8, 22 They came to Bethsaida …
>
> 8, 27 Jesus went on with his disciples to the villages of Caesarea Philippi. …
>
> 8, 34 He called the crowd with his disciples, and said to them, 'If any one wants to become my follower, let him deny himself and take up his cross and follow me …
>
> 9, 1 And he said to them, 'Truly I tell you, there are some standing here who will not taste death until they see that the

kingdom of God has come with power.'

9, 17 And someone from the crowd answered him, 'Teacher, I brought you my son; he has a spirit that makes him unable to speak and, whenever it seizes him, it throws him down and he foams at the mouth and grinds his teeth and becomes rigid, and I asked your disciples to cast it out but they could not do it.

The transfiguration passage itself is fairly coherent, if full of strange details. The text surrounding it follows on smoothly, but only if the transfiguration sequence is taken out of the equation. This is why this sequence must have originated from another source or from elsewhere in the text.

In the interpolated story, Jesus and his companions go up a high mountain. Now, the only really high mountain in the whole of the territory of ancient Israel is Mount Hermon, standing at about 9,230 feet. The range, of which it is part, dominates the surrounding landscape and it can be seen as far away as the Sea of Galilee. The ancient Herodian town of Caesarea Philippi is located at the base of it.

There is a case that the very much smaller Mount Tabor, to the south west of the Sea of Galilee, might have been intended. But it does appear from where the story has been placed, with the action beginning in the vicinity of Caesarea Philippi, that Mount Hermon was understood by the compiler of Mark to be the place where the transfiguration event took place. There is also some other circumstantial detail, as will be seen, that supports this contention.

In any case, and with either of these two mountains, the travel distances involved simply do not make for an intervening gap of six days. It is hard to find a convincing theological justification, though some have strenuously tried, for the storyteller's choice of what would be an otherwise superfluous time gap of six days (Mark and Matthew) or 'about eight days' (Luke). As an interpolation, however, the story could have had in its original context a preceding journey that would have taken six days, or perhaps even a little more.

For that, however, there are some severe geographical constraints. Israel, that is Judea and Galilee/Perea, was and is a relatively small and narrow country adjoining the Mediterranean Sea. There are few options for a journey of about a week undertaken within this territory, with any degree of focus, on foot or on the back of a mule, perhaps as much as 100 miles.

There is a possibility, however, within the text as a whole, were the transfiguration text part of the same sequence. This is the journey that is signalled, twice in Mark, as being about to take place from Jerusalem to Galilee. Jesus is given to tell the disciples (14, 28) that 'after I am raised up, I will go before you to Galilee.' And that is precisely what the young man dressed in a white robe (so, possibly a Nazorean/Essene) posted at the tomb, tells the women, that Jesus has gone ahead to Galilee, 'just as he told you' (16, 7).

However, the ending that would have filled out the details of the journey to Galilee and what may have happened there is missing from the more original shorter version of Mark, which finishes at verse 16, 8. The substituted ending in the later, longer version (with twelve verses from 16, 9-20) does not even follow the indications in the earlier text of a journey and meeting up in Galilee (1).

The distance from Jerusalem to Bethsaida is about 81 miles and, for someone still recovering from a physical ordeal, it could have taken as much as six or even eight days. The transfiguration sequence fits well as the missing text and, while this sequence could have come from some other similar source, the simplest explanation is that it is in large part the missing or 'lost' ending of Mark.

As well as providing a basis for understanding the transfiguration story itself, this identification would also explain what happened to the ending of Mark, though not at this stage why it was cut.

It should be noted that the transfiguration text does what is envisaged in Mark 14, 28 and 16, 7. Jesus is described as having gone *with* Peter (and also James and John) ahead of the other disciples who then followed on to wait for him at the base of Mount Hermon (see also pp 80 and 114).

This is an appropriate point to pause and take stock. My hypothesis, if it can be sustained, will have profound implications.

The absence of any authentic ending to the earliest gospel, Mark, has for centuries presented a barrier to analysis. The narrative of Mark, as it is, goes to verse 16, 8, thus far and no further. It offers no account of Jesus after the discovery of the empty tomb: no resurrection certainly, but no alternative scenario either. So there is and has been a problem both for Christian apologetics and for any dispassionate examination of the text.

At a very early point, soon after the gospel of Mark was first compiled or conceivably even during its compilation, I suggest that its source material was rearranged, with the journey to Galilee after the crucifixion folded back in to the text. It was placed at an appropriate point where there were other details of happenings in the vicinity of Bethsaida and Caesarea Philippi.

Relocated, it serves a different purpose and, removed from its original location, it no longer gives witness to what may well have been – in a more original version with Jewish origins – a tale of survival (see chapter 7, pp 94-102).

It should be noted that the hypothesis is not that the transfiguration sequence is a relocated story of a post-resurrection appearance, an idea that some have entertained (see pp 137-139), but that it was in its original form a continuation of the narrative that now ends abruptly in Mark. As such, it would be a piece of the post-crucifixion narrative that has been lost, a very different matter. In what follows, I will seek to examine how consistent this idea is with other aspects of the text and whether, overall, it provides the best explanation.

The authors of Matthew and Luke copied from Mark, a gospel whose ending had by that stage been truncated and, I suggest, largely removed back into the main body of the text. So, to a great extent they replicated the major dislocations present at the beginning and end of the transfiguration sequence in Mark.

These breaks in sequence may have caused as much puzzlement to them then as they do to us now.

Both authors, in different ways, amend Mark to remove the anomaly of a person in the crowd answering a statement or comment by Jesus that had, as the text now is, apparently not been made. In Matthew, a man from the crowd comes uninvited to speak to Jesus. In Luke, the man suddenly shouts out his request. In neither case, is it now a response to something that had previously been said.

Matthew simply replicated Mark's dislocated beginning, 'six days later'. But Luke, while changing the estimate of time that had passed, explained it more specifically as about eight days 'after these sayings'. What, it must be wondered, did this author think may have happened in the intervening period since the sayings, for the gap itself to be worth a mention?

My conclusion from the dislocations at the beginning and the end of transfiguration story, and its content, is that the text has been moved from another place and that the story may have been in its inception a continuation of the passion narrative.

This hypothesis has the merit of providing a plausible explanation for the otherwise inexplicable, or at least unexplained, gap of six days or maybe 'about' eight days. I offer it, however, not as speculation but as something that is supported by other evidence and that will provide a better means of understanding the text as a whole.

I have argued, both from the disjunctions at the beginning and end as well as the continuity of the text without the passage, that Mark 9, 2-16 is an interpolation. But could it be that, although a journey is indicated to a high mountain, the reference to a gap of six or eight days coincidentally refers to something else that has for some reason been omitted from the narrative? Jesus and his selected disciples might perhaps have attended a festival on the way or simply stayed with supporters or friends.

Given a starting point and destination, the reference to a time gap would of course have needed no further qualification; it simply records how long the journey took. This lends weight to the commonsense idea that this is what was intended, as opposed to some other cause whose identity and omission both have to be inferred.

There is also a framework, with missing text, into which it would satisfactorily fit. There is the journey to Galilee indicated for the lost ending, twice signalled in Mark, the disciples following on behind and even, I will argue, the detail of Peter going ahead with Jesus.

The case that the transfiguration narrative may have been relocated from an ending of Mark is thus plausible. But, if this is what happened, the text should also contain other residual clues as to its origins (see p 10) that are both mutually consistent and provide support for the thesis as a whole.

It can be seen that there are other factors that do provide such support.

'They were immediately amazed'

Although the meeting on the high mountain was supposed to be private and secret, a large crowd had learned that Jesus was there and had gathered to see him on his return. As soon as they saw him, as Mark reports, they were amazed and ran forward to greet him.

Now amazement in the gospels is a reaction reserved for apparently miraculous, or great and courageous, happenings.

There are examples in all of the synoptic gospels of the use of such terminology. Among several in Mark, the people present at the synagogue are described as being 'amazed' at his accomplished teaching (1, 22) and then again when a man's 'unclean spirit' has been driven out (1, 27).

His disciples were 'amazed' when the wind ceased when Jesus got into their boat (6, 52) after he had been walking along beside [ΕΠΙ] the lake. There was a similar reaction of amazement at the healing of the little child brought back to life (5, 42) and at the healing of the deaf-mute (7, 37).

Amazement in Mark is thus predominantly, though not exclusively, used as an appropriate reaction to miracles. But there is nothing in the story of the transfiguration that gives a reason for the crowd's amazement. It cannot be that people were amazed at the tale of the transfiguration itself, because no one had got to them to tell them about it. The crowd responded with amazement as soon as they saw Jesus. And, it might be said, Jesus' companions had in any case earlier been sworn to silence (9, 9-10).

It could be argued that a piece of text, explaining what the amazement was about, may have been 'accidentally' left out. But this really is the recourse of making the evidence fit a pre-existing position or belief; it is better to seek an explanation first for the text as it is.

There is just one powerful explanation why the crowd, rushing forward to him, should have been amazed simply to see Jesus. This is that they had, until that moment, believed him to be dead.

This would fit with the transfiguration story as a whole having been taken from an ending of Mark, possibly the ending that has been cut from the current version, and interpolated at an earlier point in the text. The crucifixion of a messianic rebel leader, following a failed revolt, would have been a piece of major news, and a disaster for most Jews – especially in Jesus' home area of Galilee. This news would have travelled back ahead of him, with the first people returning from the Passover celebrations in Jerusalem.

Having, I suggest, in an original version of the story survived the ordeal, Jesus would have actively avoided Romans, Herodians and their sympathisers on the way back to Galilee. But he and his companions would inevitably have made some contacts during the journey. The rumour that he was 'raised' spread ahead of him and as a result a 'great' crowd gathered.

It was, however, for the most of those present, second-hand news, only an unsubstantiated rumour. Nothing could have diminished the shock to the waiting crowd of seeing Jesus back there in the flesh.

It would appear that one of Jesus' first objectives, before all else, was to have a meeting with two men on Mount Hermon. He reached the villages around Caesarea Philippi but probably circumvented the town itself, which had been incorporated into the Roman province of Syria, following the death of Philip the Tetrarch.

But people had nonetheless heard that he was in the vicinity and a large, expectant crowd had gathered at the base of the mountain, waiting to see if the rumours had any foundation.

When they saw Jesus, they were, quite reasonably and justifiably, amazed.

His exile [ΕΧΟΔΟΝ] ... in Jerusalem

Whether the meeting on Mount Hermon did actually take place, or whether it was in its origins a fictional story, it raises some questions which are not easy to answer. The evidence is lacking to identify the other participants, assuming that these were not actually the spirits of ancient prophets.

It could also be that their real identities were either not known to an original witness of the event or were known and needed to be disguised. The overlaid supernatural theme draws attention away from the questions of why it was deemed necessary to have a secret meeting, involving an arduous climb up a mountain, who else might have been involved and what was the meeting's purpose.

Luke's version, though later than Mark, gives an intimation of the possibly mortal nature, in an original story, of the people whom Jesus and his companions met on the mountain. Luke's references are primarily to two men, the first of which has a qualification, almost in parenthesis, 'who were Moses and Elijah'.

Luke is, like Matthew, dependent on Mark's version, but he offers some new information, not (perhaps no longer) present in the other texts (2). This is the topic of conversation between Jesus and the two men. This is, as Luke has it, 'his departure [EXOΔON] which he was about to accomplish in Jerusalem.'

The Christian interpretation of this, which works on the basis of an understanding that Jesus' express purpose in going to Jerusalem was to be captured and die, is that EXOΔON is here a form of euphemism and refers to Jesus' anticipated and imminent death.

If the issue is looked at from another angle, that the dying-and-resurrecting god-man idea came with pagan converts into a breakaway Jewish sect and that the story had then to be made to fit, a number of issues and inconsistencies are explained.

First of all, Jesus (as portrayed, as divine) cannot be allowed to stumble, unknowing into his fate. Thus, he must be given to anticipate and announce it. On the other hand, his followers must be shown to be rather stupid, not fully understanding what he was saying, otherwise – as critics even at the time might have argued – they would then have taken steps to prevent it. Indeed, the text at other points (Mark 10, 35-37) indicates that his followers, on a course to confront the Romans, were anticipating the fruits of victory.

Having taken on a suicide mission, Jesus cannot also be depicted as having thereby put at risk his followers who might have had other ideas and were, uncomprehending, unaware of his divine plan. So, when a Roman snatch force went up the Mount of Olives and captured Jesus, quite extraordinarily no one is reported as having been killed.

The two men crucified at the same time as Jesus are described as 'lestai', which in translation has been rendered as 'thieves' or 'robbers' who thus happened to have been picked up and executed at the same time. But 'lestai' actually referred to 'bandits' and was the term the Romans used for insurrectionists. Luke even brackets Jesus with these offenders, describing them as two 'other' criminals (Luke 23, 32) (3). It does appear that the three may have been crucified as having been part of the same enterprise.

So others were in the story put at risk and may have paid the same price. The Romans were indeed not at all sparing when it came to dealing with nationalist revolutionaries. At about the same time, the Roman governor Pilate sent in forces to deal with a Samaritan messianic figure, the Taheb (Restorer), on Mount Gerizim and the outcome was a massacre.

With the transfiguration text, removed as I have suggested from an ending of Mark and reinserted at an earlier point, the late first-century compiler would have perceived that he had a problem, in that there was no record of such a story during Jesus' lifetime. He knew that, all too well. He had created it from material relating to Jesus' exploits *after* the crucifixion.

It must be remembered that this compiler would have seen his difficulties coming, not from us now many centuries later, but from people who may have had first or second-hand contact with events at the time, having survived or avoided the slaughter of the Jewish uprising from CE 66-70. These witnesses could and would have said that they knew of no such story. It is a point that the tale, as recreated, deals with; Jesus is given to tell his companions not to reveal details until after he has 'risen from the dead' (Mark 9, 9).

So this is how such informed disbelief could be countered. Jesus, as it is reported, had told people to keep quiet. So, it could be contended, no one else at the time would have known about the ghostly encounter.

But now we have a very definite instruction relating to a very definite event and still the disciples have to be portrayed as not understanding what 'this rising from the dead could mean'. Otherwise, they should have leapt into action and prevented him from handing himself (via Judas) over to the Romans.

Of course, as Jews familiar with Old Testament eschatology, the disciples would have known very well the meaning of 'rising from the dead'. The story is strained because it is adapted to an improbable course of action that it otherwise just does not substantiate.

Intimations that Jesus is made to give of his forthcoming death occur at several points in Mark, as in the other gospels, and follow a set, almost ritual format.

At Mark 8, 31, it is stated that 'he began to teach them that the son of man must undergo great suffering, and be rejected by the elders, the chief priests and the scribes, and be killed, and rise after three days.'

At Mark 9, 31, the message is repeated, 'the son of man is to be betrayed into the hands of men and they will kill him and, three days after being killed, he will arise.'

At Mark 10, 33-34, there is a further repetition, 'See, we are going to Jerusalem, and the son of man will be handed over to the chief priests and the scribes, and they will condemn him to death and they will hand him over to the gentiles. They will mock him and spit on him and whip him and kill him, and after three days he will rise again.'

The disciples are depicted as just not getting it, 'they did not understand what he was saying and were afraid to ask him (Mark 9, 32).

The mantra is of crucial importance for Christian belief and that is one reason why it is repeated. The other is to distract from what the evidence of the text otherwise indicates, a move undertaken against the Romans under cover, initially, of Jews going in great numbers to celebrate Passover. But it strains the story, makes the Nazorean followers of Jesus look incredibly and improbably stupid and has Jesus on a bizarre mission totally at odds with the historical and cultural context.

My suggestion is then that all three reports in Mark of Jesus anticipating his death derive from the Christian storyteller or editor, as conventional expressions, rather than from any earlier source. The same point can be made with respect to the similar text that has the voice of God confirming Jesus' status at his baptism (Mark 1, 11) and during the transfiguration (Mark 9, 7). In the jargon of textual criticism, these are all 'redactions'.

The Christian contention is that the word EXOΔON in Luke is a circumlocution that refers to Jesus' knowledge and announcement of his imminent death. But the best interpretation is that the other announcements have been introduced into the text, in an effort to change its direction, and that Jesus may not, in an underlying story or in any historical reality, have been actively seeking or anticipating his death. Rather, more prosaically, he was captured and crucified during a mission against the Romans that failed.

So the other references do not provide a convincing background of statements by Jesus predicting his death, into which the EXOΔON reference in Luke can be located. They are all much the same and have originated in the same way and for the same purpose.

Not only that, but EXOΔON is not a word that was customarily used either in Old Testament or contemporary Jewish sources as a synonym or metaphor for death. In fact, outside of the reference in Luke – and a derivative reference that will be dealt with in the next chapter – EXOΔON was simply not used as a substitute word for death.

There are in all some 55 usages of EXOΔON in the Old Testament which relate to such matters as the movement of people in and out of places, the movement of goods such as the export of silver and horses, the movement of stars and other heavenly bodies – hence dawn and sunset as the 'outgoings of the morning and evening', borders and fields as 'outside' and streets as ways 'out' or exits. There are no uses of EXOΔON at all as a synonym for death.

In the New Testament, there are only three uses of EXOΔON. One of these is the case in question in Luke. Another occurs at Hebrews 11, 22 where there is a reference back to the exodus in the Old Testament of the 'sons of Israel' from Egypt. A third occurs at 2 Peter 1, 15 and appears to be a derivative reference to the story in Luke (see chapter 5).

So, once again, there is no evidence of a customary use of the word EXOΔON to represent death. To find any reference that might suggest this in Jewish writings, it is necessary to go outside of the accepted (non Catholic) canon. What references can be found, as at Wisdom 3, 2 and Wisdom 7, 6, are contextual, in that they depend on an existing description or reference to death in the same context and so represent an alternative way of saying the same thing, perhaps just to avoid repetition. This is much as I might say, 'My father died and I regret his passing'.

There is however no precedent for the use of EXOΔON introduced to mean death, without any preamble to indicate that it is such a synonym, and no parallels in any case for any such use in the Old or New Testaments, independent of or aside from Luke. Given this, the possibility must be considered that EXOΔON in this case is meant literally as 'departure', 'movement away' or 'exile'.

Of course, the word does not make sense if the story is located at some point in Jesus' life, as he moves about, addressing crowds, carrying out acts of healing and gaining followers. There would have been no reason for Jesus in the story to have contemplated going into exile then.

But, seen against the hypothesis that the transfiguration is text dislocated from the ending of Mark, the use of the word ΕΧΟΔΟΝ as the topic of conversation makes perfect sense.

Jesus' confrontation with the Romans had ended disastrously. He was captured and the remnants of his followers fled. But, in a city crammed with hundreds of thousands of Jews from all over Israel at Passover and just one cohort of Roman soldiers in charge, some of his supporters sought and succeeded in contriving a situation where the crucified Jesus was taken down from the cross alive. Most crucially, the act to complete the execution, the breaking of the victim's legs with a heavy club was (according to the story) not administered.

So Jesus, I would suggest, either in fiction or in fact, after possibly a longer period of recuperation than the schematic representation in Mark allows, went ahead with three of his key supporters to Galilee. There, they held a secret meeting on a mountain with two unidentified other people, re-presented in Christian retelling as the spirits of Moses and Elijah.

What to do next? That would have been at least a major subject to consider. Jesus could hardly have gone on living openly in the confined territories of Judea/Samaria or Galilee/Perea. He would have attracted crowds and drawn the attention of the Roman and Herodian authorities. He would have been a wanted man and possibly quite easily hunted down.

His value to zealot Jews would now have been as the man who escaped. That value would entirely have evaporated, had he been captured again.

If he could no longer be an active player, then the options would have been either external or internal exile. And that is what was being suggested, his ΕΧΟΔΟΝ at Jerusalem.

There is, as matters stand, no way of telling what happened, or what is supposed to have happened, next. Jesus might have gone back to a safe place in Jerusalem or some refuge nearby, such as the Essenic community at Qumran. He could have gone outside of the country. He may have died fairly soon afterwards from wounds incompletely healed or from some other cause.

But, even if he did survive for much longer, the reason for him remaining out of sight would have remained the same. This is why what actually happened, if credence is given to the story, is consistent with what is known to be the case.

The sightings and reports abruptly stop. Jesus, for what would have been good reason, disappeared from public view.

It should be remembered that I am here simply analysing the text. The point that needs to be held on to is this. Though I have identified what accumulating evidence suggests is an underlying story, it could have been just that, a more original Jewish account, but still fiction.

What are you arguing about with ... [the scribes]?

As already noted, the end of the transfiguration story comes with Jesus descending from the mountain to find his other disciples waiting for him, surrounded by a large crowd. There is an argument going on between the disciples and some scribes.

Jesus wants to know what it is all about and asks his disciples. But this is unfortunately where the cut-in story ends and the narrative continues, at verse 9, 17 with a member of the crowd responding to something addressed to them. This, I have suggested was an address from Jesus to the crowd ending at verse 9, 1, just before the interpolation, from 9, 2 – 9, 16, the transfiguration story adapted from a continuation of the ending of Mark.

It would appear that the reply has been lost or cut. But, assuming that what is there was originally part of the ending of Mark, what *would* the scribes and the disciples have been arguing about?

Well, the disciples (that is, the 'others' besides those who had gone ahead with Jesus) were doing just what had twice been indicated to them earlier in the gospel text, at Mark 16, 7 and Mark 14, 28. They were following Jesus to Galilee. The scribes, like the rest of the crowd, would have heard rumours of Jesus' miraculous reappearance.

Doubtless, the disciples would have relished telling the scribes that Jesus had 'risen up' from the cross and was alive. That would certainly have been enough to spark an argument. The scribes would most certainly have expressed their disbelief and maybe also raised some other objection ...

And the answer to the question, 'What are you arguing about with them?' ... is, I suggest, still very much present in the text! It comes in the immediately preceding passage, when Jesus and his three companions are described as coming down the mountain together. His companions asked why the scribes say that Elijah must come first. This is in reference to the Old Testament prophecy (Malachi 4, 5-6) that God would send Elijah again, before the Day of the Lord (God) and the end times.

There is nothing specifically to indicate what may have prompted this conversation, with certainly no scribes about at that particular moment. Indeed, Jesus and his three core followers had been away from other people, apart from the two mysterious strangers, for some time.

Moments later the disciples, or at least some of them, are engaged in an argument with scribes. It could well be that the question concerning Elijah was part of their response to Jesus' own question about this argument, cut out and moved slightly back because it did not provide what a Christian compiler of the story required.

This is how the text may at an earlier point have read, on this interpretation:

> And when they [Jesus with Peter, James and John] came to the disciples, they saw a great crowd about them, and scribes arguing with them [the disciples]. And immediately all the

crowd, when they saw him, were greatly amazed and [the crowd] ran up to him and greeted him.

And he asked them [the disciples], 'What are you arguing about with them [the scribes]? Mark 9, 14-16

The disciples answered him, 'We told them that you had risen and they did not believe us. **And they [the disciples] asked him, 'Why do the scribes say that Elijah must come first?'**

And he said to them, 'Elijah indeed comes first to restore all things.'

'And how was it written concerning the son of man that he must suffer many things and be rejected?'

'But I tell you that Elijah has come [as John] and they did to him whatever they pleased, just as it was written concerning him.' Mark 9, 11-13

The text given in italics is a reasonable presumption of an eliminated piece of connecting narrative, on the basis that the interpolated text is from an ending of Mark. The implication behind the disciples' question, in what I suggest was its real context, is that the scribes were arguing that remarkable events, like Jesus' possible survival/resurrection, could not be a presage to the end times. This was because Elijah had not come again, as predicted by Malachi. Therefore, they would have maintained, contrary to all the rumours, Jesus had not actually 'risen'.

The text in bold is the immediately preceding original text from 9, 11-13, repositioned after 9, 16, where it may in a more original version have been.

What makes this interpretation so powerful is that it provides both the missing context for the discussion about Elijah and convincingly fills in the argument that some of the disciples were having with the scribes.

It is also plausible. The effect of an editor relocating the story of what happened on Mount Hermon was to turn a piece of narrative, which described what happened after the crucifixion, into something that had happened beforehand. For the change to be effective, however, any references to a 'risen' Jesus would have had to be discarded. But this would then have left the question to Jesus, about Elijah coming first, as a rather curious response to Jesus' own question about an argument the main body of the disciples were having with the scribes. Why indeed would they have been arguing at that moment, as it was relocated in Jesus' preaching and campaigning period, over the imminence or otherwise of the last days? These other disciples had no cue for such a discussion; they were unaware of anything unusual that had happened on the mountain.

So, as well as relocating the whole of the text detailing the encounter on the mountain from the end of Mark, it was I suggest also decided to put back the subject of the argument with the scribes within this text. So repositioned, it could be used, at least by implication, to serve a different purpose.

Jesus' key companions are given to recognise that Jesus was the Christian messiah, the 'Christ' (Mark 8, 29). Next, they are witnesses to God apparently giving precedence to Jesus over Moses and Elijah. Then, in another Christian adjustment, the voice of God from a cloud announces Jesus as his 'Son, the beloved'.

After this, it is of course to be supposed that the three companions would be asking Jesus if these great signs meant the coming of the end times, despite Elijah's failure to show for a second time according to the scribes.

Even discounting the objection that Elijah had, according to the narrative, just appeared again along with Moses, it is nevertheless all a bit of a bodge. Jews at the time had no conception of a Christian messiah, because there had at this point been no breakaway sect with its first members ultimately called Christians. There was certainly a messianic tradition of (very human) sons of David, rising up to throw off the shackles of foreign oppressors. The historic Jesus, from the evidence, was one of a long line of such figures during the first century.

So the acknowledgement attributed to Peter of Jesus as 'the Christ', out of time and out of context, is something that was added in, quite likely when the ending of a more original version of Mark was folded back into the narrative. The purpose of this addition was to help make the events on the mountain have a point in their new context, in a reworked narrative. The same can be said for the voice of God and the spirit appearances of Moses and Elijah, generated from what may originally have been a real meeting involving human participants.

The implicit theme is that on the way to the mountain Peter recognised Jesus as the expected (Christian) messiah. But then, having had time to think about this, on the way down the disciples raised the objection: how could Jesus be the expected messiah, given that Malachi had predicted that Elijah had to come first? Jesus' response, in this new context, was that Elijah had already returned in the person of John the Baptist.

The great problem with this, besides the fiction of Peter's 'confession', is that Malachi did not in fact predict the coming of a messiah, but *only* the coming of the last days! Jesus' Jewish disciples would have known this but not, so it would seem, the Christian editor who rearranged the text.

Jesus' 'rising up' was, however, an extraordinary event and could have been seen by those gathered at the foot of the mountain, as a sign of the imminence of the last judgement and the last days. It provided a viable context for the conversation with the scribes, at this point, and Jesus' response to it.

Hence the statement attributed to Jesus at verse 9, 1 that the end times would come about within the lifetime of some of the listeners, when they would see the kingdom of God come with power:

> **And he said to them, 'Truly, I tell you, there are some standing here who will not taste death until they see that the kingdom of God has come with power.'**

It is possible that this sentence, associated as it is with the transfiguration text, could also have been repositioned in editing and that it was, in the more original version, the concluding sentence of the sequence and, indeed, of the end of the gospel of Mark (4).

There is a case that the ending of Mark was reordered in the way that I have suggested, when it was folded back into the main text. The two references to the scribes are each, as the text now is, isolated and make little sense. But taken together, as I have indicated, these statements connect with each other and so do make very good sense.

The argument that Elijah had come, in the form of John the Baptist, met the scribes' objection that the presumed miracle of Jesus' 'rising' or survival could not be a sign of the end of times. Since Elijah had already come again and gone, in the form of John, the last days could now follow on and it would be expected that there would be accompanying miracles and great signs.

Whether or not, as I have argued, the text that I have highlighted above in bold has been slightly displaced, its form gives a strong indication of a meaning at odds with Christian interpretation.

The question that is put to Jesus is the scribe's contention that Elijah, according to Old Testament prophecy, would return again, before that 'great and dreadful day of the Lord'.

Jesus is given to agree with this formulation. But he then draws attention to another old prophecy (Isaiah 53, 3) concerning God's suffering servant, despised and rejected by men. And applies it to himself (as the son of man).

It is not, however, in this context applied as the formulaic predictions of condemnation, suffering and death, through the hands of the chief priests and scribes, which Christian writers (forbearing to mention any Romans) have subsequently introduced into the text. It is given as an example, to underline the argument that scripture has been upheld.

Thus, it was predicted that the son of man, God's suffering

servant, must suffer and be rejected. And there, as all present at the time could see, in the person of Jesus – *after the crucifixion* – was the very fulfilment and embodiment of that prediction!

The clear implication in the text is that Jesus' presence alone, bearing the scars of his suffering, is a fulfilment of prophecy, not as something that might or will happen but as something that had at that moment already happened. So also, it was argued, the prophecy concerning Elijah had been upheld in the same way, in the person of John the Baptist, 'just as it was written concerning him'.

It is only this that makes the parallel complete. Two prophecies from the past, with two sets of current or recent circumstances that fulfil them.

Just in case anyone had missed the implication in Mark, it is made explicit by the author of Matthew, who points out that Jesus was speaking about John (Matthew 17, 13).

If, however, the text is not seen as interpolated and from an ending of Mark, then the whole force of the argument is missing. The basis for the son of man's suffering in prophecy would have carried no weight, in supporting the case that prophecy has been fulfilled in respect of Elijah and John, *when it had not yet happened for Jesus*. Mark's transfiguration narrative located in a pre-crucifixion context thus lacks a convincing explanation. But, as part of the gospel's ending, after the crucifixion, the sequence from 9, 11-13 is perfectly logical and makes good sense.

Attention is drawn to a past prophecy and to its fulfilment, implied in 9, 12 as having been accomplished. The disciples are not here portrayed as unknowing, because they can see what has happened.

In Matthew, the text is changed to make it into something that it was not in Mark. The suffering/death of John the Baptist is put first. And then that is used to justify a prediction that the son of man is similarly about to suffer at 'their' (the scribes) hands.

Modified in this way, the text has now been turned from the

original issue – which was the point, raised by the scribes, that the return to life (or escape from death) of Jesus could not be a sign of the imminent last days because that depended on 'Elijah coming first', countered by the argument that Elijah had actually come in the person of John. In Matthew, that exchange hangs unsupported, having not only been removed from its proper context, as in Mark, but now also having had the sense of the rest of the conversation altered.

The coherence of the text

There is evidence of dislocations both at the beginning (9, 2) and the end (9, 16) of the transfiguration sequence in Mark. Without this sequence, the text instead of being disjointed follows smoothly on. Treating the sequence as an interpolation also resolves problems raised in seeking to interpret the pieces of challenging text, at both ends of the sequence. The phrase 'after six days' no longer need refer, and thus somehow artificially be made to refer, to what has gone before in chapters 8-9 of Mark. This is because it has come from somewhere else where the reference may well have made very good sense. There is no longer an issue of a person in the crowd responding to what Jesus has just said, when at that point Jesus has said nothing to them. This is because, without the suggested interpolated transfiguration sequence, this person *is* responding in turn, following a speech made by Jesus (5).

The interpolated sequence is quite substantial and should have left a significant gap wherever it came from. It has elements, even on a superficial level, indicating that it might have come from text that provided a follow-on to the shorter version of Mark. This version ends abruptly at verse 16, 8 despite preceding text suggesting that there is more to come in the form of a journey to Galilee, with Jesus going on ahead and his other disciples instructed to follow.

This is in outline what the transfiguration sequence provides, albeit having been moved from its original location and in the course of this quite likely modified.

The end of Mark provides an appropriate gap, from where it could have originated. There is no other convincing or even apparent location from which it might have come.

The discovery that the transfiguration story comprises in essence the bulk of the 'lost' or missing ending of Mark would resolve a major problem that has beset textual analysis and Christian apologetics for centuries. There were efforts to make good the gap from very early times. The later gospels collected and recorded stories of 'appearances' from after the crucifixion, defined according to Christian theology and doctrine as 'post-resurrection'. A writer from around the early second century provided an extra twelve verses for Mark that do not fit in terms of construction, sequence and language and are so rightly regarded by scholars as inauthentic, that is as a later elaboration.

My working hypothesis is then that the transfiguration sequence comes from an ending of Mark and that it was based on a Jewish story, oral or written, adapted by a Christian author in generating the gospel of Mark. It need not have come from the version that this author was working on but from an alternative version or some other, possibly unknown, gospel. However, the simplest explanation, which does not introduce speculative new elements, and therefore what should be the best, is that it existed as one part of a whole manuscript that was a stage in the production of Mark. This text, even if it existed only transitorily on the cutting table, would on the one hand have had a more substantial ending of Mark and, on the other, no transfiguration sequence. It is also possible that such a version was not only generated as part of the production process, but existed for a longer period in its own right (6).

As has been found, the text would have run smoothly before the ending was cut and reintroduced within it. The interpolated passage is likely to have been edited, as I have indicated, to fit its new position. There may in the more original version have been a real meeting, with the other persons present and its purpose identified. The evidence from Luke provides a clue as to what the meeting was about.

It will have been noted that, if the transfiguration sequence is better seen as a Jewish story that has been modified by Christian authors, that this could also apply to other parts of the gospels, especially the passion narrative from which it would follow. This indeed is what I have found to be the case (see chapter 6).

The theory is that the modification of an earlier text to make it fit a new doctrinal purpose will leave anomalies and discrepancies, simply because texts mesh together such that it is difficult to change one element without altering others. These anomalies will better fit the earlier text's agenda and relate better together in the context of the more original text.

That has been found with the four key elements so far identified.

The passage of six, or about eight, days has no convincing practical or theological justification in the context in which it has been interpolated. It simply makes no sense.

The same can be said for the amazement registered by the crowd, simply at seeing Jesus.

Likewise the discussion, in Luke's version, of Jesus' forthcoming exile [EXOΔON] in or at Jerusalem is bizarre and inexplicable at that point in the narrative. It was not the case that EXOΔON was used or understood as a synonym for death.

Finally, there is the missing topic of the heated conversation with the scribes. There is no reason indicated for this in the story, as it is now contrived.

All of the problematic elements make sense – and knit together – if the transfiguration sequence is identified as a passage interpolated from the ending, now missing, of Mark.

Six days to eight days have elapsed, because that is how long it took, and would have taken, for Jesus and his companions to travel from Jerusalem to Galilee, specifically the area around Caesarea Philippi. The crowd were amazed to see Jesus because reports had already reached them of the crucifixion and they had believed Jesus to be dead. The topic of conversation at the secret meeting on the mountain would have been what to do next. Some form of external or internal exile [EXOΔON] would have been among the options, possibly the only option. The scribes were arguing that Jesus had not and could not have 'risen', because such great wonders would only happen as signs of the coming of the end times – and that would only happen, according to prophecy, *after* Elijah had returned to earth again.

But, as was pointed out, Elijah could be seen as having returned in the form of John the Baptist. Thus, the carping scribes were confounded as, in the very face of Jesus' astonishing and triumphant return to Galilee, they could do no more than raise nitpicking objections.

In all of these ways, the text is more coherent if considered as interpolated, from what had been an ending of Mark, describing Jesus' journey to Galilee after the crucifixion and the events that unfolded there.

There remains the question of how the text so interpreted fits with the rest of the story. The hypothesis is that, having established the framework of an underlying text, the elements of this, including circumstantial detail, should better fit with this than with the overlaying Christian narrative.

It will be seen that it does.

The story as a whole

To start back at the beginning, at verse 9, 2, the story records that Jesus took with him Peter and James and John. He could have taken any of his disciples, and it may be purely accidental that these characters, who crop up quite often in the text, are described as being there.

However, in such a society with limited physical mobility, as in some rural communities today, ties were multiplex. So a person's friends, and so it may be said supporters, in his or her locality are likely also to have been related to him or her in some way. For someone like Jesus, as a messianic contender, there would have been a crucial divide in the roles that different types of relatives played.

Relatives by blood, in the patrilineal line, would clearly have been on his side, in the sense of being in opposition to the Romans and Herodians. But these relatives, especially brothers and nephews and sometimes even sons, were also potential rivals. When it came to conflict and military alliances, there was always at least a doubt that any such relative might take an opportunistic view of a situation. This could and did happen; it was a theme played out in the decline of the Maccabeans who for a period of over 100 years had wrested back Jewish independence. Fractrical infighting at the end damaged their ability to deal with a rising power of Rome in the region.

Among those who might have provided more reliable support were relatives by marriage and those in the female line. Such kith and kin offered a reciprocal allegiance and would not generally have been rival contenders for kingship or wealth conserved in the male line.

Those described in the gospels as Jesus' disciples or apostles represent a problematic group. There were twelve described because twelve was a significant, symbolic number and because the Nazoreans/Essenes had a central, ruling council with twelve members. But the group most certainly did not exist as described. Some of those listed appear, on analysis, to have been duplicates of each other. What is also clear is that the apostles mostly comprised Jesus' family in the male or female line and by marriage, as would have been expected in a society with overlapping ties (7).

The three people that Jesus took with him on his journey up the mountain were, I suggest, either related in the female line or loosely by marriage; they were not patrilineal kin. His supporters, James and John, were on the available evidence the children of his mother's sister, Salome. Simon (Peter) may have been related to him as the brother-in-law of these cousins, with Salome as Peter's mother-in-law (8).

They were thus appropriate as relatives who were not a potential threat and could be entrusted with political or military responsibility (9). The three do in fact appear in the gospels in a militant role. James and John, nicknamed as 'sons of thunder' (Mark 3, 17) wanted to call down fire 'from heaven' to consume a Samaritan village when their progress was blocked on the way to Jerusalem (Luke 9, 54).

Though doubtless disappointed by the response of the Samaritans, who were traditionally at odds with Jews, the story has Jesus then turning his followers away. James and John are also described, on the way to Jerusalem, as seeking positions of power in Jesus' forthcoming kingdom (Mark 10, 35), much to the annoyance of the other disciples.

The Christian explanation was that this referred to positions in heaven, after everyone was dead. The more likely explanation, in a Jewish context, is that they were jockeying for position, in the situation that would apply after the expected defeat of the Romans. Matthew even has their mother Salome (mother of the sons of Zebedee) arguing the case on their behalf (Matthew 20, 20).

Simon (Peter), the third member of the party that Jesus took with him, was certainly a pivotal figure. It was he to whom Jesus, reflecting a passage in Isaiah, gave the keys to his kingdom (Matthew 16, 19). Jesus in effect, according to Matthew, made Simon Peter his chief minister/commander. The sword-wielding Simon Peter appeared to have played a prominent role in the confrontation with the Romans at Gethsemane, cutting off the ear of the high priest's servant (Mark 14, 47, John 18, 10).

It was the same Simon Peter who is described as staying

behind and spying on proceedings after Jesus had been arrested and everyone else had fled, at undoubtedly what would have been great personal risk. Thus, Simon Peter may have been the conduit for communication, enabling a desperate plan to get Jesus down from the cross alive. He is described as denying being one of Jesus' followers, an eminently sensible course of action if there were to be a chance at all to save Jesus and himself.

Hero for his fellow Jews, Simon Peter has been portrayed as 'weak' via a Christian accounting in the gospels that follows through from the perspective of Saul/Paul, developed in his conflict with the Nazorean Jews (10).

Jesus, having suffered a defeat and been captured and crucified by the Romans and, according to the underlying Jewish account, narrowly escaping with his life, took with him three of his closest military personnel to a secret meeting. This would doubtless have been with people who were on his side, either as helpers, allies or sympathisers.

It would also appear that the three had originally been close colleagues, working beside each other as fishermen in Galilee (Mark 1, 16-20). It appears that the two families had their own boats and hired servants. These then were people with resources, wielding economic power.

For their assignation, Jesus and his three companions went up a high mountain. This, I have argued, is very likely to have been Mount Hermon, at the base of which was situated the Herodian town of Caesarea Philippi. When they got to the summit, Jesus is described as transfigured, with his clothes becoming bright white (all three synoptic gospels) and his face shining (Matthew) or changed in appearance (Luke).

Mount Hermon is certainly a high mountain, at over 9,200 feet above sea level and part of the range known as the Golan Heights. It is snow-covered at the summit for most of the year. For an upward climb of almost 15 miles, from the vicinity of Caesarea Philippi, the journey to reach the top would have taken the best part of a day. Jesus' face and clothes could well have appeared dazzling white and shining in the evening light reflected from the ground and rock face snow.

It is thus an important circumstantial detail, offered by some original witness and then altered in retelling.

Far from reading too much into the text, this is what is indicated is a parallel case where the stages, by which precisely the same thing happened, are still evident.

In the story of the discovery of the empty tomb in Mark, the women find a young man sitting down inside and dressed in a white robe (Mark 16, 5). He gives them the message that Jesus is going ahead of them to Galilee.

The author of Matthew, who used and is dependent on Mark, has generated from this an altogether more elaborate version. The young man is now an angel, 'with an appearance like lightning and his clothes white as snow'. This being gives the women the same message as in Mark. But for good measure, he has now descended from heaven accompanied by a great earthquake, rolled away the stone at the entrance to the tomb and sat on top of it, before addressing the women!

In Luke, there is not all this detail, but there are now two men dressed in dazzling clothes, again presumably heavenly beings, who so terrify the women that they press their faces to the ground.

From one version in Mark to these others, a young man's white robe has been transformed into the dazzling apparel of one or more terrifying, heavenly beings.

This is just what happened, I suggest, to a description of Jesus on Mount Hermon, a little further back in the editorial process. Jesus' face and clothes would have shone, in the early evening, with white light reflected off snow. In an initial story, this would have been how Jesus' appearance was described.

But the story was changed in retelling or rewriting and the dramatic, though natural, effect described became a heavenly transformation.

Another significant, circumstantial detail is the notice indicating that the disciples had tents with them. The long climb up the mountain would have taken a number of hours, following which there was a meeting. There might well not have been sufficient time to get back to human habitation before nightfall. Luke, indeed, has the detail that Jesus' companions were 'weighed down' with sleep and that they all came down from the mountain the next day.

Sensibly, Jesus and the disciples had taken with them their own portable tents, made of wool or hide. But it appears that the other two people there had failed to bring such equipment with them. So Simon Peter offered, as a matter of courtesy, three of these tents to Jesus and the two visitors, while presumably planning to retain one for himself and the two brothers, James and John. In the story, as it has been rendered in its new context, the visitors are presented as spirits who suddenly vanish.

It does not make sense that Simon Peter should have offered tents to spirit beings who would not have needed them.

It might also be queried how, even in a fictional story, it could be construed that Jesus' companions would have recognised the apparitions as specifically Moses and Elijah.

The author or editor of the text is clearly aware of these problems and opts to portray Simon Peter as so terrified that he spouts whatever comes into his head, a lot of nonsense. It is a convenient device, used again to try to explain away what otherwise makes no sense, of having the disciples appear as thick-witted.

But, I suggest, the Christian reconstruction is so beset with difficulties that it makes more sense to appreciate the text in a straightforward manner, with the question of tents as a surviving detail from an underlying story. The disciples took tents because they needed them. They offered these, not to spirits but to real people. What became of the offer is kept from us, because the visitors have in the relocated story been made to disappear.

There is, then, a very real underlying story that reads much better than the Christian overlay. It has the merit of hanging well together.

A final, interesting point is that Mount Hermon lies on a roughly linear route from Bethsaida via Caesarea Philippi to Damascus. Indeed, the latter two were and are the nearest significant settlements on either side of this mountain. Assuming a meeting staged at a point, more or less equally convenient for both parties, this suggests that the two men that Jesus and his disciples met may have come from Damascus.

This was at the time one of the semi-autonomous Decapolis towns or cities, which were part of the Roman Empire. It had been part of the Nabatean kingdom but was annexed by the Romans in BCE 64.

Around CE 34 or 35, there was a war between Herod Antipas and the Nabatean King, Aretas, in which Antipas was, according to Josephus, roundly defeated. The war arose from long-standing territorial disputes, but was more immediately provoked by Antipas' decision to abandon his wife of many years Phasaelis, daughter of Aretas, in favour of his own niece, Herodias.

Herod Antipas was a Roman client king. So, however, good or justifiable the grounds, the Romans would have seen Aretas' actions as a challenge. The Emperor Tiberius ordered his Syrian proconsul Vitellius to mount an expedition to punish Aretas but, before that could happen, Tiberius died.

His successor Caligula reversed the order and made a settlement with Aretas which may have included an exchange of territory. It does indeed appear that Damascus at this point reverted to Nabatean control. Municipal coinage of Damascus ceased from then on, from the accession of Caligula in CE 37, to the beginning of the reign of Nero in CE 54.

Once in control of Damascus, Aretas appointed an ethnarch as governor to rule the city (2 Corinthians, 11, 32-33). Damascus, with its chequered history, had a mixed population including a sizeable Jewish community. During the years that it then remained under Arab rather than Roman control, it provided a place of refuge for those fleeing persecution.

Acts and Saul's letters record Saul's visits to the city to seek to arrest those 'of the way'. It is a scenario borne out in the Pseudo-Clementine Recognitions, which have the 'enemy' (Saul/Paul), as in Acts 9, 1-2, pursuing dissidents to Damascus, on the authority of the high priest.

Given that Saul's independent sect for gentiles had apparently not yet been set up, it appears that the people he was pursuing were not Christians but Nazorean Jews, supporters of Jesus and of James.

Those who fled to Damascus at this time must have done so because they could find support there, not least among fellow Jews – and because it had become, not just relatively, but absolutely free from Roman control.

This suggests that there would have been Jewish zealot sympathisers living there a little earlier, in CE 36-37, when Damascus was still nominally part of the Roman domain but about to revert to the Nabateans. The Jews in Damascus may well have been prepared to offer Jesus at least covert support and advice. The mountain that lay between would have offered arguably the safest and most discreet option for a meeting place.

It would have been important to keep the details of such a meeting a secret, at the very least for the sake of the safety of Jesus' sympathisers, especially after a mission against the Romans in Jerusalem that had failed.

This would certainly explain the admonishment from Jesus to his followers 'to tell no one about what they had seen' and it may well be that this element was part of a more original Jewish narrative that provided the basis for Mark. The names of the other two participants could have been withheld or disguised, in this more original Jewish story, to protect both them and their community.

The early Christian editor retained the element of secrecy because it was helpful in dealing with the lack of recollection towards the end of the first century of any such story in Jesus' life, before the crucifixion (see also p 17). But he added the words 'until after the son of man had risen from the dead', which emphasised the placing of the repositioned narrative at a time prior to the crucifixion while reinforcing the mantra of Jesus anticipating his sacrificial death. It also served to offer a way in which the story could then have come to light.

The analysis in this chapter has pointed up the transfiguration sequence in Mark as an interpolation. There are discordant elements within it that do not fit with the story's overlaid Christian agenda and narrative and thus make no sense. But these do fit both with what would be an underlying Jewish narrative, continuing the post-crucifixion sequence, and with each other as elements of this narrative. The hypothesis has, on examination, found to be well supported by other details in the text.

My suggestion is that an ending of Mark has been modified and folded back into the text. It need not have been an ending taken from the same gospel manuscript. But this is less cumbersome, as an explanation, than having the ending of Mark cut and meanwhile an ending from some other version or even some other gospel, coincidentally introduced as a transfiguration story into the main narrative.

The choice of where to locate the story would have been dictated by what was already there. It so happened that Caesarea Philippi had been mentioned earlier (Mark 8, 27) among places where Jesus had been travelling about, preaching and possibly rallying support. So that is where the post-crucifixion narrative was relocated, out of sequence in terms of time but in terms of space in just about the right spot.

Since Matthew and Luke both replicate to a large degree Mark's transfiguration text, and were written, most analysts agree, a few decades later, this means that a version of Mark with the full ending (and consequently without the transfiguration) would have been superseded very early on. This version was thus either entirely lost or pushed to one side.

The passion narrative of Mark, as it is indicated up to verse 16, 8, and as I suggest it may have continued, is schematic, part of a sparsely told story. The reality is that Jesus would (or should, even in a fictional account) have taken some days to recover from an ordeal in which he was beaten under interrogation and left nailed to a post though his wrists for several hours. He would, or should, have then rested up in a safe house in Jerusalem.

Mark, however, has a young man posted at the tomb telling the women that Jesus 'is going', presumably imminently, before them to Galilee.

Subsequent gospel writers, without the full ending of Mark, did not have much to go on. Without this evidence, without a connected narrative, they could only report other recollections handed down of meetings or sightings.

Matthew picked up on a meeting with the disciples on a mountain in Galilee, 'to which Jesus had directed them' (Matthew 28, 16), while Luke reported encounters on the way and in Jerusalem (Luke 24, 13-40). John similarly has Jesus appear at the house where the disciples had previously met and then later by the Sea of Galilee.

These reports suggest that there may well have been two parts to the post-crucifixion narrative, a period of some days of recuperation in Jerusalem followed by a journey to Galilee.

A more original written narrative has been lost to the gospels though, I have argued, it remains in a disguised form in Mark. What readers had instead was a flimsy record, offering a confusing and fragmentary account of events involving Jesus after the crucifixion.

There are, however, some indications that on the ground, in the areas where Jesus may have lived, events were remembered and that these recollections were handed down.

It would at an early stage have been testimony at only a few removes, perhaps even from people who had known some of those who were present at the time.

The authors of the transfiguration narratives were not writing to convince us, with an eye on the situation two thousand years down the line, but for their own audiences. One of their objectives would have been to assert the theology and version of reality they were developing, against other contemporary accounts.

Chapter Five

According to Peter (again) and Saul

For I handed on to you as of first importance what I had also received: that Christ died for us for our sins according to the scriptures and that he was buried and that he was raised on the third day according to the scriptures, and that he was seen by Cephas and then by the twelve. Afterwards, he was seen by over 500 brothers at one time, most of whom are still alive though some have died.

Afterwards he was seen by James and then by all the apostles. Last of all, as to one untimely born, he was also seen by me.

1 Corinthians, 15, 3-8, late first century

I think it right, as long as I am in my tent [CKHNωMATI], to refresh your memory [of virtuous ways], since I know that the putting off of my tent [CKHNωMATOC] will come soon, as indeed our Lord Jesus Christ has made clear to me. And I am eager that, after my departure [EXOΔON], you will always remember these things.

For we did not follow cleverly-devised fables, when we made known to you the power and coming of our Lord Jesus Christ, but we had been eyewitnesses of his majesty.

For he received honour and glory from God the father, when a voice was conveyed to him by the magnificent glory, saying, 'This is my son, my beloved, with whom I am well pleased.' We heard this voice from heaven when we were with him on the holy mountain.

2 Peter 1, 13-18, early second century

If the later gospel writers had little to go on in filling out the post-crucifixion narrative, this was even more so for the author of letters attributed to Paul. While many of these are believed by scholars to be inauthentic, a core of five – 1 Thessalonians, Galatians, 1 & 2 Corinthians and Romans – show signs of having been written by the same author who may have been the same character as Saul, described in Acts. To which it may be added, this could also have been the same character as the minor member of the Herodian family Saul, as described by Josephus.

When it comes to other letters and gospels, both inside and outside of the accepted canon, the situation is still more tenuous. These were regularly attributed to New Testament characters, sometimes simply as a means of labelling or of distinguishing them and sometimes in order to make points apparently with the backing of a recognised authority.

The second letter attributed to Peter, like the first, is a pseudepigraph. It is more of a diatribe than a letter, directed against those the author identifies as 'false prophets'.

Closely following the text of the letter attributed to Jude, with sometimes even the same wording, the author is concerned to counter the disillusionment and counter doctrines that had arisen as a result of the failure of what had been seen by early Christians as an expected imminent second coming of Jesus [parousia].

The writer's chief target seems to have been 'licentious' gnostics, some of whom had begun to argue against the parousia happening as an event in the future, in physical terms. His aim was to reaffirm ecclesiastical authority (men moved by God) over individual opinion.

While the letter attributed to Paul would probably date, in an original form, from just after the mid-first century, that attributed to Peter (2 Peter) is located from its content in about the mid-second century. The earliest surviving manuscripts of each are later still. **P46**, which contains 1 Corinthians, gives the appearance of being from the second century. This leaves a substantial period in which it could, like the gospels themselves, have been edited.

The author of 1 Corinthians had no gospel account to rely on, since these had yet to be written. Moreover, as someone who had persecuted the Nazorean Jews, Saul was not fully in the confidence of family and followers of Jesus who had been witnesses of events and might have provided him with a first-hand account.

Indeed, the strains depicted starkly in Galatians and in glimpses in 1 and 2 Corinthians, as well as in the narrative of Acts, indicate that Saul had embarked on a self-appointed mission and then had come into conflict with the Nazoreans again, after telling his followers that they need no longer follow Jewish Law (Acts 21, 18-36).

This would explain why, in all of the letters that can be attributed reliably to Saul/Paul, there is so little on Jesus; no account of his life, teaching, crucifixion or of a resurrection and ascension.

Instead, Saul like the late first-century and second-century writers after Mark, had to rely on second-hand, hearsay accounts for what may have happened after the crucifixion. In the extract given above from 1 Corinthians, there is a list given of various appearances. That to Saul himself is listed last and was not as described a physical appearance, but a vision on the road to Damascus (Acts 9, 3-9).

James, the brother of Jesus, is put well down the list, as one of the witnesses. This is a reflection of the fact that Saul was in conflict with James, as leader of the Nazorean Jewish community, and would consciously or unconsciously have sought to diminish his role. The expectation is that James would have been one of the first that a risen/recovered Jesus would have met, as in the Gospel of the Hebrews.

Cephas, a name from the Aramaic for stone, most probably equates with Simon, named Peter from the Greek word for rock or stone. Peter was the key member of the group of three that Jesus is reported to have taken with him to Mount Hermon. The disciples as a group (surprisingly, since there are twelve, still including Judas) would have met with Jesus either in a safe house at Jerusalem or, in the schematic version of Mark with the end text reinstated, following on to meet him in Galilee. The five hundred could have been the crowd who had heard rumours of Jesus' reappearance, following the crucifixion, and were waiting for him when he came down from the mountain, in the story that is now cast as the transfiguration.

Whether or not the encounter reported to Saul referred to this, or to some other incident, what is interesting is the statement that some of the witnesses were still alive at the time of writing.

This would support a date for 1 Corinthians of around CE 55-60, when some of the people who had known Jesus would certainly have still been alive. It should be remembered, as I have already noted, that the authors of these texts were writing not for us, but for their contemporary audiences.

Saul must have been pretty confident. 'Look,' he was saying, 'If you don't believe me, take a boat to Caesarea and then the road to Galilee, and you will find witnesses who can back me up.'

Almost a century later on, the author of 2 Peter would have had written accounts from which to draw support, including the synoptic gospels, which included stories of the transfiguration.

It could be construed that the point in 2 Peter of introducing the subject of the transfiguration was to give credence to Peter (as supposed author of the text) in arguing for continued belief in the second coming.

So 'scoffers' are given to state, 'Where is the promise of his [Jesus'] coming?' To which Peter can be given to reply, as someone about to embrace martyrdom (as per the Acts of Peter) and as someone who had witnessed the transfiguration, that the second coming would also happen, as it is claimed he himself had foretold.

As it is relocated and reconstructed in Mark, the text has been adapted to serve the purposes of conferring approval and authority from God on Jesus and establishing his precedence over figures representing Jewish Law and prophecy. It is introduced with the sentence, with which it may originally have ended, Jesus' prediction that some present would still be alive with the coming of the 'kingdom of god'.

Throughout Mark, and thus also the other synoptic gospels which copied from Mark, the kingdom of god is portrayed, in parables attributed to Jesus, as a state that individuals could attain in their lifetimes by their good behaviour and rejection of worldly temptations. It was also characterised as the culmination of spiritual growth (Mark 4, 1-32; 10, 21-30).

Other parts of the narrative point to a kingdom that could be attained on earth for the Jews, through physical liberation from foreign oppression. This is what I argue the underlying Jewish story was about: a move against the Romans in Jerusalem by an armed force, culminating in confrontation at the Mount of Olives which ended in failure with the capture and crucifixion of the group's leader, Jesus, among others. It was how two of Jesus' key personnel, James and John, saw the situation, as they jockeyed for position on the way to Jerusalem, after what they anticipated would be the defeat of the Romans (Mark 10, 35-37).

While this underlying element has been retained, it has been qualified by the response attributed to Jesus, so as to refer to some sort of spiritual position in the afterlife.

In the Christian version, that is going to happen because Jesus is going to Jerusalem, not to take on the Romans, but in order to die.

That and the supposed reason for it, a sort of cosmic sacrifice of the god-man for man's original sin, 'a ransom for many' (Mark 10, 45) is explicitly stated. But, as with the other statements given to Jesus anticipating his death (see earlier p 44), the presumption has to be made that his disciples, though told, fail to comprehend Jesus' agenda.

Not much credence can, however, be placed on anything that Jesus is given to have said, in either a original more Jewish narrative or a Christian-adapted version, both written years after the events to which they claim to relate.

Statements about a spiritual kingdom on earth appear to have more to do with the early development of Christine doctrine, coupled with the need of this movement to draw away from anything that might suggest opposition to Rome.

Predictions attributed to Jesus of the 'desolating sacrilege' and days of 'tribulation' (Mark 13, 14-27) would have been very easy for a Christian editor to make, after the destruction of the temple and failure of the Jewish uprising from CE 66-70 (1). From the same, or a similar, hand would have come Jesus' prediction of the son of man coming 'in clouds with great power and glory' (Mark 13, 26). Just to make sure the reader knows that Jesus is supposed to think that he himself is coming back, this is repeated, in association with Jesus' response to the high priest, as reported, that he was the messiah, the son of the blessed one, 'You will see the son of man, seated at the right hand of the power and coming with the clouds of heaven' (Mark 14, 62).

Now, these expressions from the wording clearly do refer back to Old Testament prophecy of Daniel:

> I saw in the night visions and, behold, with the clouds of heaven there came one like a son of man. And he came to the ancient of days and was presented before him.
>
> And to him was given dominion and glory and kingdom, that all peoples, nations and languages should serve him.
>
> Daniel 7, 13-14

A little later in the same passage, the angel Gabriel explains to Daniel that the vision refers to the 'end of time'.

In the Christian version in Mark, Jesus is going to be the son of man coming back at the end of time. But, I have suggested that, in a more original Jewish version, Jesus' reappearance following the crucifixion is simply a sign of the imminence of the last days, with the kingdom of god coming with power (Mark 9, 1).

In the version of the transfiguration that the author of 2 Peter had, it was just an event in the life of Jesus in which he was given recognition by God and pre-eminence over the Jewish Law and prophets, represented by the persons of Moses and Elijah.

However, it is introduced with a sentence that refers to the last days, which my analysis indicates may have been the climax of the original tale on which the gospel of Mark was based and possibly, transitorily, in the template version of Mark.

It may be that this now introductory sentence provided a conscious or unconscious cue for the author of 2 Peter to use the text as means of bolstering flagging belief of early Christians in their doctrine of Jesus' second coming. The line of argument is that Peter is reliable because he witnessed the remarkable event of the transfiguration. Therefore, he is to be regarded as reliable in his prediction, as the supposed author of 2 Peter, that the second coming would still happen.

This is of course an artifice in that, from its form, content and references, 2 Peter is a pseudepigraph, dating from later than the lifetime of (Simon) Peter. Apart from which, it is tenuous to suggest that someone's word is to be relied upon because they may have witnessed something else.

It may be more than a coincidence that the story, which the author of 2 Peter has chosen to demonstrate Simon Peter's credentials, was in its original context all about the matter at issue, that is the last days and the end of time. It is curious that, in the space of just a few lines, the author has managed to include some of the story's most troublesome references.

The immediate, first parallel is with the gospel accounts that have Peter in the transfiguration story offering the ghostly apparitions of Moses and Elijah tents to sleep in. The author of Mark proposes that this was just nonsense, uttered by Peter out of sheer fright.

In the cameo in the 2 Peter letter, Peter instead refers to his 'tent' as a metaphor for his earthly body which he is about to shed, as Jesus has 'made clear' to him. It is not an unlikely choice, since the word is also used in a similar way in one of Saul's letters (2 Corinthians 5, 1), with which the author of 2 Peter indicates he was familiar (2 Peter, 3, 15-16).

The usage in 2 Peter dealt, by implication, with the questions of tents in the transfiguration story. These were not real tents taken up a mountain and offered out of courtesy to strangers, the author implies, but simply a metaphorical device.

Straight on from this, having established that he is talking about his imminent death, Peter in the letter is given to use a second metaphor for his death, that is EXOΔON, which would usually mean 'exile'. In the context, this is plainly with reference to the transfiguration story as it appears in the gospels and especially Luke, which has (still has) this term.

Furthermore, since EXOΔON is used as a synonym for death nowhere else in the canon of the Old and New Testaments and can only be found very occasionally in other Jewish writings, where the context is already established, this would seem to be a deliberate choice, made with a purpose. The aim would seem to be to counter the interpretation of the story in Luke, and possibly at the time also in Mark and Matthew, of EXOΔON as having its normal and literal meaning of 'exile'.

As if to emphasise the point, Peter next affirms that 'we did not follow cleverly devised myths' when making known the 'power' and 'coming' of Jesus, having been 'eyewitnesses of his majesty'. This most definitely makes the connection for continued belief in the return of a triumphant Jesus in the last days, on the basis of Peter as an authoritative source. The wording reflects the statement in Mark 9, 1, concerning the coming of the kingdom of God with power, that I have argued may have been part of the text when it was a continuation of the ending of Mark.

So, the contrast that is made is between the witness of Peter and his companions (hence the use of the plural 'we') and their critics who *have* by contrast, it is implied, been following 'cleverly devised myths'.

Perhaps this reference here is to the sometimes elaborate schemes of gnostic doctrine. But, linked as this is to the story of the transfiguration, it might also or alternatively have referred to a literal version of the story, set after the crucifixion. What the author of 2 Peter sought to portray as a 'cleverly devised myth' may have been an account that Jesus survived the crucifixion and then went, as is foreshadowed in Mark, back to Galilee. Even after a gap of around a century, another such version of the story might well have persisted in oral or even written tradition.

Either way, the author of 2 Peter, through the words of his eponymous narrator, is keen to debunk a view of events surrounding Jesus that challenged Church doctrine.

The author of 2 Peter rounds off the passage with a reference to God endorsing Jesus, which it is claimed Peter and his fellow disciples witnessed on the 'holy mountain'.

The critique in this letter is valuable in pointing to an alternative view, subsequently suppressed, of which we might otherwise now be unaware. What is clear is that the text's author recognised that there were some problems with the meaning of the story, and I would argue with its context, and was engaged in an effort to fix them.

Chapter Six

Keeping the Word

The transfiguration text has a lot of discrepant detail and, in the template that Mark provided for later gospel writers, gives strong indications of being an interpolation. Without the verses from 9, 2 to 9, 16, the text flows smoothly but with them, as the text now is, there are breaks in sequence both at the beginning and at the end.

The elements that do not make sense in the established context are the break of six or eight days, the amazement of the crowd at seeing Jesus, talk of Jesus' exile and the discussion of the last days involving the scribes. These would, however, fit in with each other and with their context, if the text had originated as a substantial part of the continuation of Mark after its abrupt ending at verse 16, 8, that is as part of the post-crucifixion narrative.

Other details, by this interpretation, also fit in. The two men that Jesus met could well have come from Damascus, with Mount Hermon serving as a convenient half-way point. The dazzling appearance of Jesus can be explained as starting from a description of his appearance in the evening light at the top of what was, for most of the year, a snow covered mountain.

The story, when it was moved, was also modified to serve the purposes of its Christian editors. It was adapted to convey new messages: Jesus' pre-eminence over Jewish Law and prophecy and God's affirmation of his status. But the starting point, the motivation for taking the text out of the ending of Mark, is likely to have been developing Christian doctrine.

The question is: what would have been of such pressing concern, within a relatively short time after the compilation of this gospel, that its ending had to be cut?

The author of Matthew based his text on Mark, and was written most scholars agree not much later than the beginning of the second century. Yet Matthew offers nothing suggesting that he had the cut ending available, as a source. What he does provide is both short on detail and curiously vague:

> Now the eleven disciples went to Galilee, to the mountain to which Jesus had directed them. When they saw him, they worshipped him, but some doubted.
> Matthew 28, 16-17

The trip to Galilee is twice signalled in the remaining text of Mark. Its appearance in Matthew has the hallmarks of an intelligent projection, as opposed to being a summary of what had been in Mark.

If Matthew had used a subsequently eliminated ending of Mark, then there should have been more detail, just as there is with other parts of the narrative that he has used. If he had, moreover, the ending available then he would, from what has been deduced was in it, have distinguished between the disciples who went with Jesus to Galilee and the remainder who followed on afterwards.

The uncertainty over whether the person encountered was Jesus is a theme that also appears in Luke in the story of the meeting on the road to Emmaus (Luke 24, 13-32) and in John in the stories of Mary and the gardener, 'doubting' Thomas and the miraculous haul of fish (John 20, 14; 20, 25; 21, 4).

This theme of doubt and uncertainty over whether Jesus had actually reappeared is something that was a factor in a second phase of the development of a Christian narrative (see p 129).

It does seem that, in the absence of a reliable ending, or even any ending to Mark, the other gospel writers made up for the gap in the best way that they could, with scraps of remembered testimony handed down over the years.

But the outcome could then and now be seen to be unsatisfactory. No one, neither with the twelve verses later added nor with the rewrites attributed to Matthew, Luke and then John, has ever managed to generate a good substitute for the missing ending of Mark.

The early editor of Mark, who rearranged the text, for whatever reason preferred the abrupt termination of the storyline, with the tomb empty and the women fleeing in fear.

But he left in the references at verses 14, 28 and 16, 7 indicating that there was a continuation in which Jesus went on to Galilee. In the more original Mark, the 'risen' Jesus had to make, as foreshadowed in the text, a substantial journey. And, for that, he would in a recovering state have needed help.

So it looks as if the text immediately preceding the now-missing ending may have been amended, at the same time. Jesus would have needed to be accompanied on his journey to Galilee. But the text as it now is excludes this detail. Moreover, it reads very oddly. Why should it have been construed that the young man posted at the tomb told 'his disciples and Peter' of Jesus' journey ahead of them, when Peter *was* one of the disciples?

The origins of such a clumsy form can be seen if the text had originally read, before being amended, or just rearranged, as 'But go tell his disciples that he is going with Peter ahead of you to Galilee'. This would fit in with the missing ending that has been deduced. Moreover, the text, even as it now is, can be read in this way:

> ΑΛΛΑ ΥΠΑΓΕΤΕ ΕΙΠΑΤΕ ΤΟΙϹ ΜΑΘΗΤΑΙϹ ΑΥΤΟΥ ΚΑΙ ΤѠ ΠΕΤΡѠ ΟΤΙ ΠΡΟΑΓΕΙ ΥΜΑϹ ΕΙϹ ΤΗΝ ΓΑΛΕΙΛΑΙΑΝ
> (lit) But go tell the disciples of him, 'Also with Peter, he goes before you into Galilee.'
> Mark 16, 7

KAI is commonly used in New Testament Greek as a conjunction to link words and phrases or introduce sentences. While the best translation is often 'and', the word can also, depending on context, have such meanings as 'also', 'moreover' and 'then'.

In this instance, 'with' or 'also with' seems most appropriate, even if a scarce usage, and makes more sense in the context than 'and'.

The translators of Codex Sinaiticus online perceived the problem of using 'and' for KAI in conjunction with 'his disciples' and have translated KAI here as 'and especially', an even more unusual usage that would appear to have no precedent and creates a new problem. Why would Jesus in the storyline have singled Peter out by telling the women, 'Go tell his disciples and especially Peter ... ' There is nothing in the context that provides a reason for taking such an unusual interpretation.

Taking KAI here as 'with', by contrast, is suggested by context. An injured and recovering Jesus would have needed someone, or some other people, to go with him to Galilee, both to sustain and protect him (1). The text that I have argued has been relocated as the transfiguration story bears this out. According to the narrative, Jesus went to the mountain in Galilee with Peter, James and John.

The text, in the truncated end of Mark, indicates that the disciples should follow on to find Jesus in Galilee. The transfiguration narrative has them doing just that, waiting for him at the base of the mountain.

I have argued, on a number of grounds, that the transfiguration sequence from Mark 9, 2-16 is better seen as having originated from an ending of Mark and then been modified and reintroduced back into an earlier point in the text. I have identified points at which Christian editors appear to have changed an underlying Jewish text.

While it is not the purpose here to analyse the gospels as a whole, it is my contention that Christian writers and editors did regularly adapt both oral and written Jewish texts and stories to suit their purposes. Analysis shows that they often kept quite a lot of the more original material. This was partly because they had to make do with what they had. There was only limited source material available.

It was also because any change tended to lead to complications; other parts of the text then had to be modified (or should have been, in some cases) for the sake of consistency.

An additional reason for retaining as much of the original as possible may, however, have been an almost reverential respect for anything surviving from Jesus' time and context. This ran in parallel with a ruthless disrespect for its actual meaning.

The text was sacred because it was to do with Jesus. But 'the Jews', who had produced it, had clearly got it wrong. These people, the followers of James, were the ones who had humiliated and driven out Saul; they were the enemies, false prophets and false teachers whose teachings had to be repudiated.

So, the sense could be altered with impunity, to serve a purpose – and divine inspiration would ensure that the editors' new version would be correct, the word of God. The word, though rearranged would be kept, as much as possible.

Such conceptual schizophrenia was an inevitable consequence of the fact that Christians needed the Jewish context (Jesus was a Jew), while at the same time rejecting Jesus' Jewishness, and also the Nazorean Jews who followed him and his brother James.

It is evident at many points in Saul's writings, which preceded the gospels, for example in the First Letter to the Thessalonians:

> For you [the Thessalonians] suffered the same things from your fellow-countrymen as they [the churches in Judea] did from the Jews who killed both the Lord Jesus and the prophets and persecuted us/drove us out. They [the Jews] displease God and oppose everyone by hindering us from speaking to the gentiles, that they may be saved. Thus, they [the Jews] have constantly been filling up the measure of their sins. But

> the wrath [of God] has come on them at last.
> 1 Thessalonians 2, 14-15

However obvious this may be, it has still to be pointed out that it was the Romans who executed Jesus and it may well be that a majority of Jews at the time did support, or would have supported, him.

The double-edged approach of Saul and the early Christians comes out clearly in the Letter to the Romans:

> As regards the gospel, they [Israel/the Jews] are the enemies [of us, or of God], in respect of you. But according to election, they are beloved because of their ancestors/ancestry.
> Romans 11, 28

A few years after Saul, Christian writers were freely rearranging the writings of their enemies and claiming, at the same time, that their new versions better represented the truth.

To demonstrate how widespread the practice was, here are two other examples, the first from John. While the text appears to have been only relatively lightly edited, this has left a couple of huge inconsistencies and a host of circumstantial detail indicating what the story may originally have been about:

> And on the third day, there was a wedding in Cana of Galilee and the mother of Jesus was there. And both Jesus and his disciples had been invited to the wedding.
>
> When the wine gave out, the mother of Jesus said to him, 'They have no wine.'
>
> And Jesus said to her, 'O woman, what [concern] is that to you or me? My hour has not yet come.'
>
> His mother said to the servants, 'Do whatever he tells you.'
>
> Now, there were standing there six stone jars for the Jewish rites of purification, each holding twenty or thirty

gallons. Jesus said to them, 'Fill the jars with water.' And they filled them up to the brim.

He said to them, 'Now draw some out and take it to the chief steward.' So they took it.

When the chief steward tasted the water that had become wine and did not know where it had come from (though the servants who had drawn the water knew), the chief steward called the bridegroom and said to him, 'Everyone serves the good wine first and then the inferior wine, after the guests have become drunk. But you have kept the good wine until now.'

Jesus performed this, the first of his signs, in Cana of Galilee, and revealed his glory and his disciples believed in him.

After this, he went down to Capernaum with this mother and his brothers and his disciples and they remained there a few days.

John 2, 1-12

The first glaring anomaly is Jesus' reply to his mother, which in the context would have been an extraordinarily rude put-down. This I suggest may have been a comment initially removed from elsewhere, possibly the story of the woman taken in adultery (John 7, 53; 8, 1-11). In what may have been its original context, the reply would have revealed too much (2).

The second anomaly comes from the fact that Jesus' mother and Jesus himself, apparently just guests at the wedding, were called upon or took it upon themselves to resolve a major catering crisis. The chief steward, also aware that the wine was out, would in such circumstances have deferred to the mother of the groom, or possibly of the bride.

That should then have been what he did. Jesus then fixed the problem. Then, the chief steward congratulated the bridegroom.

This, I suggest, would have been Jesus, who had provided the extra supply of wine (albeit possibly from the residues of what had run out, heavily diluted with water), without having to account to anyone except his own mother.

It was thus, on this reading, Jesus' own wedding and in his home territory of Galilee. Jesus' mother was the mother of the groom to whom the chief steward deferred. Jesus was the bridegroom.

Could he really, as a mere guest at a wedding, have taken control and ordered the servants to put a large quantity of water into the empty, or nearly empty, stone jars? (3). This is without having the politeness to tell 'the bridegroom', if someone else, whom it must be supposed the servants also neglected to inform and who had failed to notice the problem. This could hardly be the case, it must be said; the wine had actually given out and 'they' (the guests) had 'no wine'.

It was a very large wedding, judging by the quantity of reserves of water-turned-into-wine, as would have befitted a major figure, a messianic contender for the throne of David.

Jesus was there as part of a large party, including his mother, his disciples and it would seem his brothers. This indicates that they were major participants.

Direct references to the bridegroom and the bride by name have been cut, as has Jesus' reply to his mother that might have clarified his role.

John reports it as the first thing that Jesus did, so also I suggest part of what (Mark 1, 38) he came out to do, from his seclusion until adulthood among the Nazoreans.

The motivation in this case for the alterations to the text would have been Christian squeamishness over their semi-divine messiah having sexual relations and a family, as any or least most normal Jews (4).

I am not suggesting that all this, taken together, amounts to a proof that this text was in its origins a description of Jesus' own marriage (5). However, my interpretation for this text does have the merit of explaining the anomalies, omissions and other circumstantial detail better than any other theory that I can conceive at present. Moreover, this is just one of many examples, some of which are discussed here and others elsewhere (6), forming an identifiable pattern, where an underlying Jewish story has been modified for doctrinal purposes.

The second example, which comes from Luke, is much more heavily disguised and I would argue relates to Jesus' initial entry into the zealous Jewish, Nazorean movement, which then both protected and educated him. It is the only story, from among the canonical gospels, relating to Jesus' childhood:

> Now, every year his parents went to Jerusalem for the festival of the Passover. And when he was twelve years old, they went up as usual for the festival.
>
> When the festival was over and they started to return, the boy Jesus remained in Jerusalem but his parents did not know this. Assuming that he was in the group of travellers, they went a day's journey. And then they were looking for him among their relatives and friends.
>
> When they did not find him, they returned to Jerusalem to search for him. After three days, they found him in the temple, sitting among the teachers, listening to them and asking them questions. And all who heard him were amazed at his understanding and his answers.
>
> When his parents saw him, they were astonished; and his mother said to him, 'Son, why did you treat us like this? Look, your father and I were anxiously searching for you?'
>
> And he said to them, 'Why were you searching for me? Did you not know that I must be about my Father's business?'
>
> But they did not understand what he said to them.
>
> Luke 2, 41-50

The ostensible point of this story is to show that Jesus got his knowledge and understanding, not from other men, but miraculously. It was God-given, so that even as a child he was ahead of the elders and religious teachers at the temple at Jerusalem, without apparently anyone having had to tell him anything.

Thus, a little later in Luke (Luke 4, 16-22), Jesus is given to return to Galilee and read and preach authoritatively from the book of Isaiah in the local synagogue. Those present were depicted as impressed, though wondering a little how this could have come from 'Joseph's son'.

But Luke's story is taken from Mark 6, 1-3, where the situation is described much more graphically. The people wonder, 'Where did this man learn these things? What is this wisdom that has been given to him? What miracles are being done by his hands?'

They do not even seem fully to recognise him, 'Is this not the builder [TEKTωN], the son of Mary and brother of James and Joses and Judas and are not his sisters here with us?'

This story, related in Mark, Matthew and Luke, is not at all consistent with Luke's other tale of Jesus at twelve years old, outsmarting the temple preachers at Jerusalem. There were many other people in the group from Galilee, such that it could have been supposed that he was lost among them. The tale of his adventure and his demonstration of remarkable ability would have thus been known to a number of people and would have spread. His prodigious talent, developed still further, would have become common knowledge by the time that he was an adult.

So, there is no explanation for the reaction of total amazement – quite plainly related in Mark and Matthew and only a little watered down in Luke – at Jesus, back in Galilee as an adult, reading and interpreting scripture. He was very talented and this had apparently been recognised early on. So everyone would or should have known that.

The key is that the incident involving Jesus reading at the synagogue occurs at an early stage in the narrative. Jesus is in

Galilee and the people there, who would have known him as a child, no longer recognised him.

Jesus had been away, most probably with some or all of his brothers, not just for three days but for several years. He would have stayed among the Nazoreans, which is how he became described as a Nazorean leader, under their protection with his brothers, away from the attentions of Romans and Herodians seeking out would-be messianic contenders. His sisters, since there was no threat to them, would have stayed behind (Mark 6, 3).

The Nazoreans had an organisation with remarkable parallels with people who are presumed to have lived by the Dead Sea at Qumran, where they left behind scrolls describing their way of life and beliefs. Described as 'Essenes', these people described themselves in other ways, as 'the poor', like the Ebionites ['evyonim' meaning 'poor ones'] who succeeded the Nazoreans as followers of James. The coincidences are so great (7) that it may be that 'the poor' at Jerusalem and at Qumran were one and the same. They might alternatively have been loosely linked, with parallel messianic aims and organisation.

One of the ways in which the organisation recruited new members was by adopting young men who had reached the transition point to adulthood, at around 13 when boys celebrated their bar mitzvah. So Jesus, who became a Nazarene, could have been adopted into the Essene/Nazorean community in Jerusalem – and that is where he would have acquired his scriptural learning.

Jesus 'came out' (Mark 1, 38) of the organisation, it would appear for several reasons, to take up the mantle after John the Baptist had been killed, to recruit followers and to preach, and perhaps, as is suggested by his first great 'sign' at the very beginning of John's gospel, to marry.

There are many examples that I could have chosen to demonstrate the widespread modification of underlying Jewish stories and texts. The two illustrated here are from the defining points at the start and finish of a period, in respect of which the gospels and other Christian sources are silent and when Jesus was actually absent from the general community.

The tale in John, I suggest, originally told of his marriage feast, the remarkable scale of it and how Jesus saved the situation when the wine ran out. Jesus' true role was, albeit imperfectly, elided because the Christian Jesus could not be married.

The tale in Luke had, as its source, the oral tradition or knowledge that Jesus and his brothers had been harboured during their youth and young adulthood among the Nazoreans, as was their custom and as was in fact necessary for the safety and well-being of this particular group of siblings.

The author of Luke included a greatly modified version of this, partly to make the case that Jesus was divinely inspired, rather than humanly taught and partly to counter what was still known, that he had been brought up among an extremely religiously zealous Jewish messianic group. There for maybe as much as ten years or longer, some said. Not so, was and is the line in Luke, it was just three days.

I have suggested that the narrative throughout the gospels has, as its basis, one or more original Jewish sources that have been amended to suit Christian doctrinal purposes. The transfiguration story is particularly interesting because it also shows signs of being an interpolated text and having originally been part of what would have constituted an ending of Mark. Without this ending in Mark as their prime source, the authors of Matthew and Luke had to use what material they had, which may in both instances have been oral tradition.

In Matthew, the scant reference to a meeting on a mountain 'to which Jesus had directed' the disciples (Matthew 28, 16) could reflect what had survived in recollection of the meeting described in an original ending of Mark. This, I have argued, was taken out and folded back into the main body of the text to become the transfiguration episode.

In Luke, the fragmentary passed-on memories related to a period after the crucifixion, when Jesus was in the vicinity of Jerusalem. There would have been, in reality or as an element of a convincing story, a necessary period of recuperation before Jesus could make his journey to Galilee. This, though it would or should have happened, is missing in the schematic account, with the transfiguration narrative restored to its original place, in a more original version of Mark.

The type of analysis that I have undertaken here can, of course, be applied to other parts of the passion narrative or to this narrative as a whole. While I have attempted this elsewhere (8), I propose to summarise some of the key points in the next chapter.

The passion narrative is interesting because analysis indicates that it was, in its original form, a tale not of death but of survival.

Chapter Seven

Death in the First Century

The climax to the gospel accounts naturally divides into two parts. The first part provides a description of the journey from Galilee to Jerusalem undertaken by Jesus and his followers, in the run-up to the festival of Passover. This results in a clash on or near the Mount of Olives with a force sent out from the city to intercept them, resulting in the arrest of Jesus and possibly some others.

The second part of the narrative deals with the interrogation, trial and crucifixion.

The Christian interpretation of the first part is that Jesus went to Jerusalem with the objective of being taken and crucified, though conceding he may have had some second thoughts, in the expectation that God was going to raise him from the dead.

There are certainly a number of elements that would reinforce such a view, including repeated statements accorded to Jesus of what was going to happen, misunderstood by his loyal but rather simple followers. I have referred to these above. They follow a defined pattern and stand out as Christian additions to an underlying narrative.

The objections to the Christian construction are manifold. It is logically inconsistent and also at odds with the historical and cultural context, as well as with other elements in the narrative. At a time when rebellions were regularly taking place and just as regularly brutally put down by the Romans, it has to be supposed that one of the would-be messianic Jewish liberators (the Jew's own king, even according to Pilate), had actively sought failure and death.

There are, as with other cases discussed, many traces indicating an underlying Jewish narrative, at odds with the

Christian account. The swords that Jesus urged his followers to buy (Luke 22, 36), the fracas (or battle, downplayed) that took place on the Mount of Olives, in which weapons were used, the capture and crucifixion of two other 'bandits' besides Jesus and the gathering in Galilee (Matthew 17, 22) followed by the move on Jerusalem are all indicative that what was originally described was, at least as a story, an insurrection.

Why should any such details have been left in, when these were at odds with the narrative reworked to serve a Christian purpose? The reasons, already suggested, were both practical and polemical. If too much is cut, it diminishes the story. While major amendments require modifications elsewhere in the text, for consistency, these are sometimes simply missed. Most of all, the Christian editors were writing for an audience around the end of the first century, when there were people living who had met witnesses to the events. So there would have been strong, recently-generated oral traditions.

The way to counter these effectively at the time would have been to defuse, rather than deny them. So, yes, Jesus and his closest inner circle met two men on a mountain. But these were the ghosts of Moses and Elijah. Then, of course, there may have been talk of tents and exile. But this (2, Peter) was all to do with intimations of mortality and death.

And Jesus as a child did spend some time with the 'elders' in Jerusalem. But this was just three days and not a number of years. He went as an adult to a wedding and played a prominent part in the proceedings. However, it was not his but the wedding of some other, unspecified person.

In the same way, it could be granted that a great band of Jesus' followers gathered and went armed to Jerusalem. But the swords they had, in the story, were just tokens.

There are, interestingly, some clues in the narrative as to what really went wrong with the uprising. In the first place, it appears that Jesus may have been provoked or stirred into action before he was fully prepared by reports of yet another Roman atrocity. 'There were some present, at that very time, who told him about the Galileans whose blood Pilate had mingled with their sacrifices' (Luke 13, 1).

This would have been in Jerusalem since, in a religion centred on the temple in Jerusalem, that is where Jesus' fellow Galileans would have made their sacrifices. The historical event that this may refer to was a massacre in which soldiers, on Pilate's orders, attacked a crowd protesting at the sequestration of temple funds for use in building an aqueduct (*Antiquities* 18, 3, 2). When Jesus had been captured, it is reported that there were already in prison rebels, including Barabbas (son-of-the-master/father) 'who had committed murder during the insurrection' (Mark 15, 7).

Having set off from Galilee, perhaps insufficiently prepared, the next problem that Jesus and his followers encountered was active resistance from Samaritans through whose territory they had intended to pass. Jesus sent messengers ahead of him, but his way was blocked, because of his intent on going to Jerusalem. They had therefore to go round a longer way (Luke 9, 52-56).

If Jesus had been expecting support, this would have been a setback. On the other hand, the Samaritans had their own religion and expected a messianic figure, the Taheb, and were traditionally at odds with the Jews. If this were towards the end of Pilate's rule as procurator, there might well have been an additional reason for the Samaritans' nervousness. They were about to stage a demonstration on Mount Gerizim, which Pilate subsequently did put down with such great brutality that it may have been the cause for his recall to Rome.

At such a sensitive point, the Samaritans would have wanted to avoid gratuitously provoking the Romans. They may have calculated that allowing Jesus and his followers through their territory, on the way possibly or evidently to launching an insurrection in Jerusalem, would have been regarded as complicity.

So, they prevented it.

Once at Jerusalem, overlooking the city from Gethsemane at the Mount of Olives, Jesus is described in the gospels as being in a state of great anxiety. He called on his key followers, several times during the night, to stay awake and keep watch, chiding them each time they fell asleep.

Now the Christian gloss, in the story, is that this was due to Jesus having second thoughts about delivering himself up (through Judas) to die at the hands of the Romans.

But why the repeated insistence on his key followers staying awake and keeping watch?

A much more plausible explanation, and the reason that Jesus was in such a state, with sweat in the red light of dawn falling from his face like drops of blood (Luke 22, 44), is that he was looking for help, for reinforcements that, for whatever reason, never came.

There are indications of what sort of problem Jesus and his followers faced. But the story is short on, or has been shorn of, useful details.

The second part of the passion narrative deals with Jesus' trial, crucifixion and then 'rising', with the predicated journey back to Galilee now missing, or as I have argued now misplaced, back in the narrative.

What is quite extraordinary is the weight of direct and circumstantial detail in the text indicating that Jesus could have survived and did survive the crucifixion. The underlying Jewish narrative provides the information that Jesus, in the sense that we would now understand it, did not die. This is something that has to be carefully qualified because the writers of the underlying account, approaching two thousand years ago, may in this respect have had a different way of seeing the world.

The evidence can be divided into elements that (a) provide direct or circumstantial support for the theory that the more original *story* was that Jesus survived and (b) countervailing arguments and detail indicating that Jesus must have died.

An uncompleted execution

Crucifixion was, as well as being an intended form of torture, not a clearly defined way of causing death. What actually caused death in most cases by the (relatively) 'quick' method was the blow from a heavy iron club to break the legs (crurifragium), causing the victim to sag and die from the combined effects of suffocation, caused by his own unsupported weight making it difficult to breathe, shock and loss of blood.

In the slow method, the victim was left on the cross, with his weight supported, to perish primarily from hunger, thirst and exposure after a period that could amount to several days.

In the quicker method, failing to break the victim's legs would have been more or less equivalent to neglecting, in an execution by hanging, to pull the lever that operated the trap door.

The central point is that what was being described was an execution which involved exposure and public humiliation, followed by the act that actually killed the victim. In the story, even as amended, the fatal blow was not delivered. Why did the Christian editors, who adapted the earlier Jewish narrative, simply not change the text? They could have had Jesus executed in another, more reliable way. Or they could have inserted a sentence or two describing a Roman soldier swinging the crurifragium club.

The point that applies equally to this, the transfiguration and other gospel stories is that they were writing not for us, but for an audience that had recent information and would likely have been aware that Jesus' legs were not broken.

In the synoptic gospel accounts, there is no description of a soldier going to break the legs of the crucifixion victims and the failure to deliver the fatal blow is implicit. In Mark's account, Pilate had to summon the centurion to find out if Jesus were already dead, when 'Joseph of Arimathea' (Mark 15, 42-44) requested the body. In Luke and Matthew, Pilate simply allowed Joseph to have it.

John had a Roman soldier, on discovering Jesus apparently already dead, refrain from breaking his legs but instead thrust a spear into his side. Outside of an attempted harmonisation, there is nothing that can be found to support this in the earlier synoptic gospels (1). So, while the author of John could have had some separate and reliable source, the reference to the spear wound may well have been included to counter objections, arising from the accounts in earlier gospels, that Jesus' execution had not been completed. The implied suggestion is that, even if the fatal blow with the club was not administered, the spear thrust did in any case kill him.

Evening up the odds

Coincidentally or otherwise, the trial and execution were contrived (against the provision of Jewish Law) to take place on one day, on the eve of the Sabbath and Passover. Perhaps not so coincidentally, the proceedings were dragged out by a degree of prevarication, such that when Jesus was finally put on the cross there were only a few hours to go to sunset, the start of the Sabbath, when the bodies would according to custom have to be taken down.

So Jesus was not nailed on the cross by his hands (or, more likely, wrists) for very long. He should, as a fit man used to walking long distances and in his prime, not have died from the combined effects of this and the abuse he suffered under questioning.

According to the story, he did not have to endure carrying the heavy cross piece to the place of execution; someone else, Simon of Cyrene, did that for him. It could be said that this simply indicated that Jesus was in too weak a state to carry the cross piece, having been severely beaten. However, it can also be argued that the outcome was actively brought about, so as to conserve his strength and improve his chances of survival.

Jesus was not crucified in a public place, according to the gospel of John, but in a garden, where there was a new tomb. The other gospels do not mention a garden, but do refer to the tomb and the place of execution as Golgotha, claiming that in Hebrew this meant 'place of the skull'.

But, in Hebrew, Golgotha is better translated as something like 'stone press', an item that would have been useful in extracting oils from herbs, and perhaps an actual or colloquial name for somewhere that was in fact a garden.

The execution took place in unusual circumstances. Passover was the most significant of three festivals – the others being Pentecost and Tabernacles – that Jews were required to attend at the Temple in Jerusalem. So the city would have had a vastly swollen population from a level of around 40,000 to perhaps 250,000 or even more.

There may have been just one cohort of Roman soldiers, about 500 to 600 men, stationed in Fortress Antonia, overlooking the Temple. The rest of Governor Pilate's troops, as many as 2000, were at his headquarters at Caesarea, too far away to be of much use in an emergency.

Pilate could have agreed to have the crucifixions of Jesus, and the two other 'bandits', staged in a more private place, with the aim of avoiding trouble. His brief would have been to maintain public order, while avoiding major disturbances if at all possible.

Notwithstanding the effectiveness of the Roman soldiers as a fighting force, they could in the circumstances have been overwhelmed by sheer weight of numbers. Indeed, at the beginning of the first Jewish uprising thirty years later, in CE 66, the Roman garrison was forced to surrender, and then massacred.

Pilate was thus in a relatively weak position, and so was the detachment of soldiers sent up to finish off the crucifixion victims. In a confined space of a private garden, and faced with a probably hostile crowd pointing out that Jesus was already dead, they could have decided, as the story has it, not to break the legs of this particular victim.

A private garden with a rock tomb would, in addition, have provided a perfect setting to stage-manage an execution from which the victim could be rescued. Concealed within the tomb would have been the men who worked on Jesus from the Friday night, until he was fit enough be taken out, as per the gospel of Peter (Gospel of Peter, 36-39). One young man was then posted to tell any supporters or well-wishers who turned up at the tomb where Jesus was going next and so where he could be found (Mark 16, 6-7).

A simulated death

Before crucifixion, Jesus was offered a drink of wine and myrrh, presumably a combination intended to deaden pain (Mark 15, 23). The wine would have had some effect in this respect and so would the myrrh, which has been found to be a mild analgesic.

But Jesus refused the mixture. This meant that he would still have had his wits about him later, to take vinegar offered to him on a sponge, following which he either immediately died or lapsed into a state resembling death.

The vinegar should not have generated this effect. It would instead have acted as a mild stimulant.

It is suspicious that Jesus, a fit and healthy man, should have died at this particular point, with no apparent, immediate cause of death.

So, is there anything in the text that could clarify the situation? It would seem so. In the gospel of Peter, what is described as having been offered is not simply vinegar but a mixture of vinegar and 'gall'.

Now, gall is commonly taken to mean a bitter-tasting substance, but in Hebrew the word used for the opium poppy *was* gall [rosh]. This, then, was what was offered to and accepted by Jesus on the cross, according to Peter. It could, if derived from the juice of the poppy, have induced almost immediate unconsciousness. A sufficient dose would have caused the victim to fall into a coma, a state that would to many people, then and now, have closely resembled or been indistinguishable from death.

It would have been a very dangerous state to be in, but necessary if the objective were to create an impression of Jesus as collapsed and already dead.

Matthew has subsequently confused the issue by suggesting that what was offered to Jesus *before* crucifixion was not wine and myrrh but wine and gall. However, this author has derived his material from Mark and consistently modified and elaborated it. He appears here to have substituted 'gall', that is opium, for myrrh.

The executioners would not have seen it as useful, by administering opium, to induce a state of complete unconsciousness in a victim just before crucifixion. What is more, this is not what the narrative indicates had happened.

The author of Matthew has thus got his story wrong. He probably 'borrowed' the idea of gall [rosh] from somewhere else. I suggest that it would, as it still is in the gospel of Peter, have originally been in the later part of the narrative of Mark that deals with the drink offered up on a sponge to Jesus on the cross.

It was, I suggest, relocated from this part of the narrative in generating the gospel of Matthew and at the same time, or about the same time, eliminated from Mark.

The implication in Peter is that the opium was given to Jesus to hasten his death. But Peter has the wildly unlikely scenario that it was not the Romans but the Jews who were crucifying Jesus. Furthermore, the Jews confusingly had only just 'commanded', it has to be presumed the Romans, 'that his legs should not be broken, so that he might die in torment'.

The author of Peter was clearly striving to deal with the problem of how to explain why the drink of vinegar and opium was offered, not as a matter of routine by the executioners, but at a later stage, by a 'bystander'. He suggests that there was suddenly an unnatural darkness for three hours from noon, and that therefore there was a switch from desiring to torture Jesus to wishing to kill him quickly so that he could be taken down before the Sabbath.

While the canonical gospels also mention this three hours of unnatural darkness, they do not suggest that people were at all concerned about it. On the contrary, it was only later, when evening was really about to fall, and following the administration of the vinegar or vinegar and opium, that there was a move to take down the body before the Sabbath.

The unnatural darkness I suggest derives from Amos 8, 9, 'on that day, says the Lord God, I will make the sun go down at noon and darken the earth in broad daylight.' Not an extraordinarily coincidental eclipse, which in any case would only have lasted a few minutes, this probably derives from the pesher-style construction of Mark using Old Testament prophecy (2). But in this instance the prophecy was not related to an event that did occur, or might have occurred, at the time. It was simply stuck in, while casting about for suitable prophecies that could apply to the circumstances of Jesus' crucifixion.

The author of Matthew, I suggest, cut out the later reference to opium with the vinegar given to Jesus on the cross and then balanced this up by substituting opium for the myrrh with wine that had been offered earlier.

The author of Mark would, I suggest, have had no problem in including the opium (rosh), as part of the mixture offered on a sponge. It would have made sense in the context of the ending to the gospel that is no longer present. The opium [rosh] may therefore have been there originally in Mark and then subsequently cut.

Counter-indications

There is an apologetic argument that Jesus died because of the effects of his mistreatment, most notably a severe beating meted out by the Romans on the orders of Pilate (Mark 15, 15).

Persons condemned to crucifixion were indeed sometimes subjected to a horrific ordeal, in which they were beaten with a whip of leather strands imbedded with pieces of metal. It was an additional punishment, especially reserved for slaves. It caused such huge damage that the victim often died from it and what was then nailed up on the cross was a bloodied corpse. For the convenience of the executioners, such beatings were carried out at the execution site. This was so that the victim, while still able to walk, could be got there unaided and without undue trouble.

The gospel accounts indicate (Mark 15, 15, Matthew 27, 26, Luke 23, 22, John 19, 1) that the 'scourging' to which Jesus was subjected took place instead during or just after his examination by Pilate, as part of the process of interrogation.

This was a very much milder procedure, a beating with rods, a means either of extracting information and confessions or perhaps a way of warning the innocent and guilty alike not to cross the authorities. As Luke has it, Pilate proposed simply to 'chastise' Jesus before releasing him, having found him innocent of any capital offence.

Following his scourging, Jesus is depicted as walking and standing and being led away, certainly not collapsed or in a state of collapse.

Paul/Saul claimed in his letters to have suffered such beatings many times and this is borne out by the account in Acts. So the scourging, as described in the gospels, should not have been sufficient to cause Jesus to die, without having had his legs broken whilst on the cross. He appears from the narrative to have been at least as fit as Saul. His treatment should not have killed him.

A further argument is that Jesus could have been crippled by being nailed to the cross through his feet, which would have had the dual consequences of helping to hasten his death and making it difficult or impossible for him subsequently to travel to Galilee, on foot or on the back of a mule. Moreover, assuming that he did get there, he should not then have been physically able to walk up and down a mountain, even after a delay of several days or weeks.

However, the only direct references in the gospels, including Peter, are to Jesus being nailed through the hands. So, in John, the 'doubting' Thomas is invited to put his finger in the wound and see Jesus' hands. In the gospel of Peter, the 'Jews' are described as plucking the nails from Jesus' hands on taking him down from the cross. But, again there is no mention of nails in feet.

However, in Luke, the disciples are invited to look at Jesus' hands and feet, which does at least imply that he had suffered wounds to both.

Victims were sometimes tied to a cross and it is possible that Jesus may have been nailed by the hands or wrists and tied by the feet.

The evidence taken as a whole, I suggest, points to an underlying Jewish narrative in which it was proposed that Jesus was crucified but survived, largely through the efforts of his supporters. They managed, in the story, to influence the circumstances of the crucifixion, contrived a state that very closely resembled death and then worked hard to revive and sustain Jesus, after he had been taken from the cross.

That certainly is the story. I am not at this point considering whether the events happened as described, whether indeed these were anything like historical fact.

But what was the purpose of the story, together with the continuation in Mark that was originally there? Why was this, in Christian editing, folded back into the text and modified to become the story of the transfiguration?

How the 'good news' was constructed would have depended

on one's perspective. And, around CE 55, two radically different perspectives were beginning to emerge in respect of the same narrative.

So, first of all, there is the question of how Jews may have viewed the stories of Jesus' return to Galilee, as it circulated and as it was in one version encapsulated in a prototype of Mark. Then, there is the question of how this may have looked to the new 'Christians', once Jesus was elevated to the status of a god.

The framework of the story could not contain both versions, just as Judaism could not contain its emerging, turbulent sect, was in consequence stretched to breaking point, and then broke.

Here first, is the story of what happened to the Jewish Jesus.

Chapter Eight

Day of the Lord

It is difficult to assign dates to the interrelationship between John the Baptist and Jesus. This is because the evidence, outside of the gospels, for an historical Jesus, is slim and because there are contradictions in the accounts of John.

Precise dating is fortunately not essential for present purposes. What follows is a summary outlining what may be the best fit.

There is no reference to Jesus in Josephus' account of the Jewish uprising against the Romans from CE 66-70, the *Jewish War*, written around CE 75. A Slavonic version has a description of Jesus that is discordant with Josephus' style and beliefs, suggesting that this was an addition made later, by another author.

There are two direct references and one indirect reference to Jesus in Josephus' history of the Jewish people, *Antiquities*, written in CE 93. Jesus is mentioned directly in a story concerning an illegal stoning, carried out in CE 62 by a hastily convened Sanhedrin, while there was no Roman governor in place. The victim, James (Jacob, in the Greek) is described as 'the brother of Jesus who was called the Christ'. It seems possible that this originated as a marginal note, inserted by a commentator seeking to match Josephus to the Christian story, which was then incorporated into the text when it was recopied. There is also some doubt whether this James/Jacob was the same James/Jacob who operated as an opposition high priest, was the brother of Jesus and was murdered at the outset of the war, a few years later.

The other references to Jesus do help to establish a timescale. Pilate ruled as procurator from about CE 26-37, when he was recalled to Rome following a series of misjudgements.

The culmination of these were an assault on Jews, protesting against Roman sequestration of temple funds to build an aqueduct and then finally a massacre of Samaritans assembled near Mount Gerizim in support of their messianic leader, the Taheb. Following the first of these incidents, there is a description in *Antiquities* of Jesus as 'a wise man' who 'wrought surprising feats' and who 'was the messiah'. This again does not ring true as authentic comment by Josephus and seems to have been a later Christian interpolation.

Its placing, however, is interesting, especially as it is immediately followed by two, gossipy tales that *do* read as authentic Josephus, as parodies of the Christian stories and of Saul's activities in raising and then allegedly misappropriating funds from diasporan Jews (1).

Immediately following these two tales is the account of the massacre of Samaritans at the foot of Mount Gerizim.

The positioning of the interpolation and the Christian parodies, before the Samaritan massacre and after the clubbing of Jewish demonstrators in Jerusalem, gives an indication of timing. What it suggests is that the author/authors of these passages were aware that the events surrounding Jesus occurred towards the end of Pilate's procuratorship, possibly as late as CE 36.

It is indeed possible that Jesus' move on Jerusalem, under cover of Passover, was part and parcel of the temple funds incident. There is a description in Luke 13, 1-5, of Jesus being told of fellow Galileans 'whose blood Pilate had mingled with their sacrifices', which could have provided a reason for his deciding to take on the Romans (2). At Mark 15, 7, there is a similar telling reference to 'Barabbas' who 'was among the rebels in prison who had committed murder in the insurrection.'

Barabbas [son of the master or father] appears to be a characterisation or label, rather than a proper name. It would have fitted Jesus. The Jewish crowd may thus have been demanding not the crucifixion, but the release of their messianic leader.

Either way, these traces from another story suggest that the confrontation with the Romans entailed more injury and loss of life than are allowed for in the gospel accounts.

The analysis of the evidence relating to John the Baptist also indicates a date for the crucifixion, if an historical event, of around CE 36.

In the gospels, John's activity precedes, and is part of, what instigated the campaign ('ministry', in Christian terminology) by Jesus. In *Antiquities*, Josephus describes how the ruler of Galilee and Perea, Herod Antipas divorced his longstanding wife, Phasaelis. This was in order to marry his niece, at the time married to his half-brother Herod, described as 'Philip' in the gospels.

Phasaelis' father, Aretas, king of neighbouring Nabatea, was already in a border dispute with Herod Antipas. As a result of this and the insult to his daughter, he decided to launch an attack across the border. In the resulting battle, Herod's army was routed.

According to the gospel accounts (Mark 6, 17-29), John the Baptist had also criticised Herod Antipas for taking his brother's wife, while his brother was still alive. John had been imprisoned by Herod, supposedly for this criticism, and then beheaded as the result of scheming by Herod's wife Herodias and step-daughter Salome. Central to this was the demand, on the basis of an open promise, for the head of John the Baptist.

But it would appear that John was more than just a wild man in the desert. According to the account in *Antiquities*, Herod Antipas had captured and killed him as a pre-emptive measure to forestall a possible popular uprising. Josephus here also commented that some believed that the destruction of Herod's army was divine retribution for the way John had been treated.

There are now some clear pointers to dating. John's death came first, followed by the battle between Herod Antipas and

Aretas. There is an Arab tradition, which supports this sequence, that Herod had sent John's head to Aretas to warn him off from taking action.

If this actually happened, then it can only be said that it proved ineffective. Aretas did attack and Herod Antipas was defeated. After he had been defeated, Herod wrote a letter of complaint to the Roman Emperor Tiberius. The Emperor then wrote to the Syrian Governor Vitellius ordering him to wage war on Aretas.

Vitellius was appointed in CE 35 and Tiberius died early in CE 37. At this point, Vitellius had taken his troops to Jerusalem but, with the death of the Emperor, he pulled back from invading Nabatea.

This sequence suggests that John the Baptist was probably killed in CE 34 and there was a brief but decisive battle, in which Herod Antipas was defeated, around the beginning of CE 36.

John could not have been killed much later because this would have left insufficient time for the conflict, the complaint and then consequent order to Vitellius, followed by the death of Tiberius. It could not have been much earlier because it is clear, from gospel accounts, that John had also objected to the marriage of Herod Antipas to Herodias. This marriage was the event that precipitated the war with Aretas.

The gospel story of Salome's dancing, used by her scheming mother to bring about John the Baptist's death, provides a further indication that this dating is correct. Her husband (and uncle) Philip the Tetrarch died in CE 34, following which she would have taken up residence in the household of her step-father, Herod Antipas. But it would not have been for long, since she was next married to another Herodian, Aristobulus, possibly the kinsman of Saul/Paul mentioned in Romans.

If Jesus took over from John in late CE 34, then this leaves just sufficient time for the events described in the gospels leading up to his capture and crucifixion in CE 36.

The gospel passion narrative thus relates to events that are presumed to have taken place in CE 35-36. I have demonstrated that the transfiguration story is an interpolation and provided a detailed case, indicating that it was in original form a continuation of the gospel of Mark. But it was early on modified and folded back to a point earlier in the text. It was in this way that the ending of Mark was lost.

I have also shown that the underlying Jewish story, supported by many crucial details, was that Jesus had survived.

It is possible that this was simply a story, with no basis in fact, told either for its dramatic effect or possibly to give consolation to Jews over what would have been yet another failed attempt to defeat and dislodge the Romans.

The way the text was constructed shows, as will be seen, that there was more to it than that. Moreover, there are indications that there was a factual basis. It would, for example, have been pointless, only a few years after the time to which the story relates, to have created and circulated a story contradicting events, whose course and outcome were generally well known. In addition to which, Saul was able, around twenty years or so after the crucifixion, to claim eyewitnesses to Jesus' reappearance (1 Corinthians 15, 3-9). This was some time before the first gospels came into circulation.

It may also be relevant that the later canonical gospels, though lacking an earlier and more original ending of Mark to help them, were able to provide disjointed fragments from oral testimony that had by then have been passed down one or two generations.

The evidence, which was examined in the previous chapter, indicates that it was feasible that Jesus could have survived. The underlying story of survival that can be seen in Mark may thus have had some basis.

There would, it is worth noting, very soon have been at least *two* Jewish versions of what had happened to Jesus.

One would have been what was known by his family and

fellow Nazorean helpers, who had revived him, got him from the tomb, helped him recuperate and then provided a safe place to hide for the long term. This then would have been the internal exile, ΕΧΟΔΟΝ, in or near Jerusalem that was being discussed in Luke's relocated text.

Jesus was evidently never tracked down and at some point would have died from natural causes. He would have probably died well before the end of the Jewish uprising and the mass suicide at Masada, because by then he would have been about 80 years old. After which point, following the wholesale destruction inflicted by the Romans, there would have been few surviving witnesses as to what had really happened.

My suggestion is that, assuming Jesus did survive the crucifixion, what had happened to him and his whereabouts would have been a secret, well kept for many years. This is because of the very real threat he would have faced from the Roman and Jewish Sadducee authorities had he resurfaced and been recaptured.

Jesus would have been in his forties at the time of the crucifixion, having been born by most calculations around BCE 6. Given that life expectancy was not nearly as great as nowadays and given the trauma of his ordeal, Jesus may not have survived very long after his ordeal and subsequent reappearance in Galilee.

This supposition is certainly consistent with the fact that nothing further was heard from him.

Around three decades later, members of the new breakaway Jewish sect were looking for evidence for a Jewish figure who had been subsumed by gentile converts into the framework of their existing pagan beliefs. The pesher-style story that they unearthed then provided the basis for the gospel of Mark.

This had at least some correspondence to what the Nazoreans knew, assuming the historicity of Jesus, but would have been kept from Saul.

Another version of events would have arisen from the eyewitness accounts of those who had heard of Jesus' crucifixion from other Jews returning from Passover and then witnessed his astonishing reappearance days, or more probably weeks, later at the foot of Mount Hermon. These, I have suggested, provide the source for material incorporated in later gospels, after the ending of Mark had been lost.

Given that the details of what really happened had to be kept secret, and secrecy was certainly a theme (Mark 9, 9) even as the story has been transformed into a Christian narrative, there would have been scope for the story of Jesus' reappearance at Mount Hermon to have grown in retelling into something that was not merely extraordinary, but miraculous. But as that remarkable performance was it, as Jesus had just vanished and the years passed and nothing further happened, there was also scope for doubt to creep in. Those among a diminishing band of surviving witnesses must have wondered whether or not the person they had seen really was Jesus.

The Christian account, which I will examine in the next chapter, would therefore have had two prime sources for the passion narrative, used in two stages. One was the Jewish tale that was modified and used in creating Mark, some years after the crucifixion. The other was passed-down oral testimony, brought in to help provide a completion for the other, later gospels. This latter testimony does exhibit the qualities that I suggest might well have crept in with the passage of time, a tendency to place a miraculous interpretation upon events, accompanied at the same time by increasing doubt.

Prior even to the passion narrative, however, the newly emerged Christians had a pre-existing pagan framework into which a spirit Jesus, by Saul's account appearing to him in dreams, could be welded.

Our understanding of the Jewish original story is based on a Christian version mediated as the gospel of Mark. I have concluded that the transfiguration, in its un-remodelled form, had been an account of the journey to and events in Galilee, twice signalled in the text of Mark, but lost when the ending that had been there was cut. While this account could have been part of some other version, in another manuscript, which provided a continuation of the passion narrative, it is hard to envisage why it should have happened in this way. The simplest and best explanation is that, when the ending of Mark was cut, it was folded back at an appropriate point into the main body of the text. It was, at the same time, modified so that it could serve a different purpose.

It has to be acknowledged that some of the editing may have happened at an early point and that there could have been, and probably was, other editing of the main body of the text.

It seems reasonable to offer a suggestion of how an ending of a more original Jewish source for Mark might have looked, bearing in mind that there could have been text deleted that left no trace and so cannot now be reconstructed.

First, for purposes of comparison, here is the ending with the twelve verses which most experts agree were subsequently added:

> As they (the women) entered the tomb, they saw a young man, dressed in a white robe, sitting on the right side, and they were amazed. He said to them, 'Do not be amazed; you are looking for Jesus the Nazarene, who was crucified. He has been raised; he is not here. Look, there is the place where they laid him. But go, tell his disciples and Peter that he is going ahead of you to Galilee. There, you will see him, just as he told you.'
>
> And they went out and fled from the tomb, for terror and amazement had seized them.
>
> And they said nothing to anyone, for they were afraid.

> Now, after he rose early on the first day of the week, he appeared first to Mary Magdalene from whom he had cast out seven demons. She went and told those who had been with him, as they mourned and wept. But, when they heard that he was alive and had been seen by her, they would not believe it.
>
> After this, he appeared in another form to two of them, as they were walking into the country. And they went back and told the rest but they did not believe them.
>
> Later, he appeared to the eleven themselves, as they sat at table. And he reproached them for their lack of belief and hardness of heart because they did not believe those who had seen him after he had risen.
>
> And he said to them, 'Go into the whole world and preach the good news to all of creation. Whoever believes and is baptised will be saved but whoever does not believe will be condemned. And these signs will accompany those who believe: they will cast out demons in my name, they will speak in new tongues and they will pick up snakes with their hands. And, if they drink any deadly poison, it will not harm them. They will lay their hands on the sick and they will become healthy.'
>
> So then the Lord Jesus, after he had spoken to them, was taken up into heaven and sat down at the right hand of God. And they went out and preached everywhere, while the Lord worked with them and confirmed the message through the signs that accompanied it.
>
> Mark 16, 5-20

The story without these verses, or some other ending, is clearly incomplete. It reaches the point where Jesus has been crucified and the tomb is empty, leaving open the questions of what happened to the body and whether Jesus, naturally or miraculously, might still be alive. The story builds to a climax and that climax, in the abbreviated version that ends at 16, 8, is missing.

The argument, that the verses in the longer ending were nonetheless a later addition, was put by Bruce Metzger in *A textual commentary on the New Testament*. In terms of the narrative, Metzger makes the telling point that verses 9-20 of the longer ending do not follow smoothly from the previous text; there is a severe dislocation. The subject of the final verse of the abbreviated Mark is the women who ran away, afraid. The subject of the first verse of the longer ending, denoted as 'he', is presumably Jesus. If the narrative had been continuous Jesus should, for the sake of clarity, at this point have been named.

Mary Magdalene is introduced in the opening sentence of the longer ending as if she were a new character, with a qualifying comment 'from whom he had cast out seven demons' to define her. But she had already been introduced to the reader, having been mentioned twice in the previous few verses.

In the longer ending, there is no mention of the other women described in Mark 16, 1-8, Mary the mother of James and/or Joses and Salome, although this might have been expected, had this really been a contemporaneous continuation.

The plot is left unresolved at the end of verse 16, 8 and the sentence is left hanging. The final clause, ΕΦΟΒΟΥΝΤΟ ΓΑΡ [for they were afraid] is highly unusual as a means of ending a sentence or paragraph.

The women kept silent, except perhaps to tell the disciples, as instructed. But the reader is not told why they were afraid. A clause beginning with 'because' is almost invited at the end of 16, 8 after 'they said nothing to anyone for they were afraid'. The wording of the beginning of 16, 9, 'Now, after he had risen on the first day of the week', does not relate to the previous text. It is unsuited as a continuation.

The added verses, as a whole, do not deal with the climax that is indicated. Peter and the disciples are told to go to Galilee, which presumably they would then have done. But there is no mention in the additional text of the disciples making such a journey or its outcome. There are descriptions of other appearances or meetings. But the only one that is indicated, from what has survived of the original ending of Mark in the shorter version, that is a journey to Galilee, is not dealt with in the additional verses.

The language and style of the longer ending, Metzger points out, are different in some ways from the text of the abbreviated Mark.

The word 'Lord' [KYPIOC] is used twice in the last paragraph, even though this usage is alien to Mark while frequently used in the later gospels.

Some content, such as the appearance to two persons, appear to be summaries of, rather than a source for, material in Luke. The reference to 'seven demons', with regard to Mary Magdalene, appears in Luke 8, 2. Other elements, including the use of speaking in tongues as a sign, may well have originated from Acts.

The longer ending is thus not even remotely convincing. It is a later addition.

In the following, I have added Mark's transfiguration text minus miraculous elements, with the two men that Jesus and his companions met on the mountain treated as real but human, with Luke's additional contribution as to what they may have been talking about included and also with the KAI TΩ ΠETPΩ [and or with Peter] in the preceding text interpreted positionally, so as to make better sense.

> As they [the women] entered the tomb, they saw a young man, dressed in a white robe, sitting on the right side, and they were amazed. He said to them, 'Do not be amazed; you are looking for Jesus the Nazarene, who was crucified. He has been raised; he is not here. Look, there is the place where they laid him. But go, tell his disciples that he is going with Peter ahead of you to Galilee. There, you will see him, just as he told

you.'

And they went out and fled from the tomb, for terror and amazement had seized them.

And they said nothing to anyone [except the disciples], for they were afraid.

[Jesus set out to Galilee] and, after six days, took Peter, James and John and led them up a high mountain, privately by themselves.

And his appearance changed before them and his clothes became a dazzling white. And there appeared to them [two men] who were talking with Jesus. They were speaking of his ΕΧΟΔΟΝ [exile] which he was about to accomplish in Jerusalem.

Then Peter said to Jesus, 'Rabbi, let us make three tents, one for you and one for [us] and one for [the two men].

And, as they were coming down from the mountain [on the following day], he ordered them to tell no one what they had seen.

And when they came to the disciples, they saw a great crowd about them, and scribes arguing with them [the disciples]. And immediately all the crowd, when they saw him, were greatly amazed and ran up to him and greeted him.

And he asked them [the disciples], 'What are you arguing about with them [the scribes]?'

[The disciples answered, 'We told them you had risen and they did not believe us.'] And they asked him, 'Why do the scribes say that Elijah must come first [before the day of the Lord/last days]?'

And he said to them, 'Elijah indeed comes first to restore all things.'

'And how was it written concerning the son of man that he must suffer many things and be rejected?'

'But I tell you that Elijah has come [as John] and they did

> to him whatever they pleased, just as it was written concerning him (3).'
>
> And he said to them, 'Truly, I tell you, there are some standing here who will not taste death until they see that the kingdom of God has come with power.'

It can be agreed that this reconstruction does involve an element of surmise. What it does point up, however, is how inadequate the longer ending is and how well the essential elements of the transfiguration narrative fit as a continuation of the text in Mark leading up to verse 16, 8.

I demonstrated that the transfiguration text in Mark is where it now is, as an interpolation. So, having conceded that some leaps have to be made in putting the narrative back to make a coherent whole, I will now concentrate on the very end.

Here, I certainly do not concede that my conclusion (pp 49-53) that verses 9, 11-13, must originally have come after verse 9, 16, as shown above, is at all hypothetical.

As it stands, or rather stood, the text would be a garble. Jesus asks a question about what appears to have been an important and maybe crucial discussion that had been taking place, and there is no answer to it.

But, just a few verses previously there has been a discussion, apparently apropos of nothing, that precisely answers that very same question and is absolutely spot on as an answer, in the context of Jesus' return to Galilee, after having survived ('risen' from) the crucifixion. It has been very slightly displaced (4) from where it had been: following on from Jesus' question to his disciples, having found them, on coming down from the mountain, engaged in a heated discussion with some of the scribes, part of a very large crowd.

Even in Mark's rather terse rendering, it is a quite extraordinary scenario.

Jesus and his companions have been up on the mountain overnight, for a meeting, to which Peter and the brothers James and John were sworn to strict secrecy.

The crowd, alerted to his coming, must have gathered and waited for many hours. Some of the scribes were among them, perhaps expecting to see an end to a preposterous rumour.

Then, down came Jesus, bearing the scars of his crucifixion, with the crowd, utterly amazed, scrambling and falling over themselves to get to him.

The scribes were utterly crushed. The argument that Jesus was about to make is embodied by his reappearance. Here, before their very eyes, was the fulfilment of scripture.

This, I contend, is how the gospel of Mark originally ended. It is in fact a well-crafted completion to a story that was about something very much other than the later Christian preoccupations that have been grafted on to it.

It was based on a Jewish narrative. And it was about the last days.

The story began at the very beginning in Mark, as it can now be seen to have ended, with a reference to John the Baptist, as the messenger of God, sent to prepare the way for the coming of the Lord God:

> As it is written in the prophet Isaiah:
>
> Behold, I am sending my messenger ahead of you, who will prepare your way;
>
> a voice crying out in the wilderness, 'Prepare the way of the Lord; make his paths straight.'

This is actually a combination of two quoted passages, The first part is from Malachi (5) which at verse 3, 1, foretells that the Lord of hosts will send a messenger to prepare his way, and then at verse 4, 5 makes it clear that this would happen through the return of Elijah:

> Behold, I am going to send you Elijah the prophet before the great and terrible day of the Lord.

The second part is a direct reference to Isaiah 40, 3, whose reference to a voice crying in the wilderness is thus linked in Mark both to the coming of last days and to the appearance of John the Baptist 'in the wilderness'.

As far as the Jews were concerned, the signs were there, in the form of a series of failed uprisings and terrible atrocities committed by the Romans at the beginning of the first century. The end times were surely coming. John was seen, at least by some, as having been – if not Elijah himself – then the embodiment of the spirit of Elijah.

As Luke 1, 17 has it (quoting Malachi 4, 6), 'And, with the spirit and power of Elijah, he [John] will go before him [the Lord their God] to turn the hearts of the fathers to the children, and the disobedient to the wisdom of the righteous, to make ready for the Lord [God] a people prepared.'

Or, as Matthew 11, 12-13, even more tellingly describes it, in words attributed to Jesus, 'From the days of John the Baptist until now, the kingdom of heaven has suffered violence and men of violence take it by force. For all the prophets and the Law prophesised until John prophesised; and, if you are willing to accept it, he is Elijah who is to come.'

So, John is seen as Elijah (at least, by some) in his second coming. The day of the Lord (Malachi 3, 1-2; Joel 2, 1; 3, 14; Zechariah 14, 1) was thus at hand.

Who were the 'men of violence' who had taken the kingdom by force? It is hard to find any other convincing candidates besides the Romans, Herodian rulers and the collaborating Sadducee high priests together with their enforcers which included, it would appear, at one point Saul/Paul (6).

With John as an expression on earth of Elijah, the next event that might have been expected was a sign signalling the imminent day of the Lord. This is where the second thread of prophecy comes in, this time in relation to the story of Jesus. He is given, in the story, to see himself as a manifestation of the suffering servant who in the words of Isaiah 53, 3-9, would be 'despised and rejected by men', like a lamb 'led to the slaughter'.

The implication is that this was the sign of the coming last days, God's chosen one, Jesus, 'risen' from crucifixion, the suffering servant restored and justified. Isaiah, it should be noted, anticipated that the Lord's servant would survive to 'see his offspring', 'prolong his days' and 'see the fruit of the travail of his soul and be satisfied'.

The more original ending of Mark, as here reconstructed, provided a framework for belief in the end times, in the face of possible counter arguments. So, while some believed that John the Baptist may have been, at least in spirit, a form of reincarnated Elijah, he himself had reportedly (John 1, 21) denied it. What is more, at the time of Jesus' crucifixion and reappearance, John had been dead for only a short time, perhaps as little as two or three years. He was not some long-gone figure, easy to mythologise, but someone that people had recently known, warts and all. Charismatic certainly, but as people had known him, he was very much human. The common memory of the Baptist may thus have clashed with a Jewish theological imperative.

Mark's purpose, as originally expressed in its underlying Jewish narrative, may then not have been to deify Jesus. It was to use the example of Jesus to reaffirm the prophetic role of John and so thereby confirm the coming of the last days.

The startling reappearance of Jesus, the suffering servant restored, is given to demonstrate the power of prophecy. Just as Jesus, despised, rejected and making 'his grave with the wicked', had ultimately come, as Isaiah had predicted (so it was argued), 'to prolong his days', so also the prophecy with regard to Elijah was fulfilled in the person of John.

Mark goes full circle from the coming of John, in fulfilment of prophecy at the beginning of the story, to his life and his role vindicated at the end by the experience of Jesus' reappearance, the last great sign.

The day of the Lord really was at hand.

It was and is a crackingly good story, carefully fashioned from prophecies set against actual events that took place, or were believed to have taken place or that may in some respects (such as the darkness over the land) have been pure fiction.

It is also a very old story, dating to the mid-first century and to the concerns of the people at that time, and Jewish in its origins. It had little to do with Christian perceptions of Jesus that then developed over the next few centuries.

I suggest that it operated on at least two levels. It offered the promise of spiritual redemption in the last days for Jewish believers who called 'on the name of the Lord (God)' (Joel 2, 32). It also offered the prospect of the Lord God going forth to battle on their behalf to destroy their enemies and restore his kingdom on earth (Zechariah 14, 1-21).

The narrative of Mark told the story of prophecy fulfilled, with John the Baptist as the embodiment of Elijah and the restoration of Jesus as the sign of the last days.

This was not written to make Jesus into a god or present his suffering as some form of sacrifice for mankind or to create a new theology. These themes have originated as Christian interpretations and overlays.

It should be remembered that the Jewish story that is the basis of Mark has an accumulation of detail indicating that Jesus could have survived. Given the desperate situation in which Jesus was placed in the story, however, his rescue and successful recuperation would nevertheless have been taken as an almost miraculous event.

While the stand-off with the Romans on the Mount of Olives had been a disaster, a shambles, Jesus' actual or claimed reappearance later was at the very least a great propaganda coup. It must have raised spirits and perhaps roused others to take action.

The last days, presaged in the original of the transfiguration story for Mark, operated and could be taken on more than one level.

With the help of the Lord God, the Romans would be defeated. A long-lasting Jewish kingdom on earth would be established, with the Romans of course necessarily expelled.

It could possibly be the end of time, with God's judgement visited on the wicked and with the righteous taken up into heaven.

On either view, Jews who had kept the covenant would be rewarded, while the 'kings of the earth' would be broken 'with a rod of iron' (Psalm 2, 9).

It is part of the elegance of what, I have deduced, constituted the essentials of the ending of Mark that it does operate on several levels. It projects belief and a religious agenda. It is also in part politically subversive.

I suggest that the story may have first originated, rather like the Commentary on Habakkuk and Commentary on psalm 37 peshers from the Dead Sea Scrolls, (7) in an effort to interpret, against existing Jewish scripture, and project from a series of events. The life and fate of John, was interpreted as God sending his prophet Elijah again to prepare for the close of the age and day of judgement. Roman atrocities were seen as part of the turbulence expected from 'men of violence', prophesied to accompany the last days. The miraculous 'rising' of Jesus [Yeshua] was regarded as a sign of what was about to happen.

The problem for Jews was that nothing did happen. Or, rather, what had been predicted failed to happen. The Jewish kingdom of God on earth was not established. Far from being defeated, the Romans crushed the Jewish uprising from CE 66-70, inflicting death and destruction on a massive scale. The temple, the centre of Jewish worship, was destroyed. There was no redeeming, final judgement day.

The wicked appeared still to prosper and go unpunished, while the righteous were not visibly rewarded.

The Nazoreans were damaged, as were all Jews, by the disruption and loss of life. But they had also provided at least the zealous heart, and possibly even active support, for the anti-Roman messianic movement. They and their successors, the Ebionites, who revered James and saw Jesus as a great prophet, were indelibly associated with this calamity.

When the Ebionites later failed to support the Bar Kokhba uprising in CE 132, they became even further marginalised, and their numbers dwindled further.

Their story failed even to find a place in Jewish literature. It survived only in a form, rearranged by Christian writers to serve a different purpose.

Chapter Nine

Second Coming

According to the timescale established in the previous chapter, Jesus would have been crucified in the early part of CE 36. Saul, reinvented as Paul in letters attributed to him and in Acts, would then have been interacting with James, other relatives and supporters of Jesus during the period following of over twenty years.

These people formed the Nazorean community in Jerusalem, even though the family of Jesus had their roots in Galilee. The two biblical sources, Acts and the letters, agree that Saul came on to the scene after the crucifixion and never encountered Jesus, except in visions or dreams.

There is nothing in Saul's letters indicating that he was aware of Mark or any of the subsequent gospel accounts or indeed of what may have been in a Jewish prototype for Mark. He offers no biographical details, no sayings, no accounts of any miracles and some fairly terse references to Jesus' crucifixion (1). It is clear that all such accounts were either written later or, in the case of a pesher-style analysis of the fate of Jesus set against prophecy, was inaccessible at the time to Saul.

Yet the people whom Saul was seeking to join, and with whom he then came into conflict, would or should have known what had happened to Jesus. That is assuming that Jesus had existed and was an historical character, from the same time period, and that he was one of the group that included James.

What the narrative as a whole indicates did happen to Jesus was not revealed to Saul. Therefore it must be deduced that either James and the others did not tell him, or that that they did not know because the passion story was a subsequent invention.

I have argued that there is good reason to believe that Jesus did exist and that the Jewish story of his survival may have had a basis in fact.

But, if this were so, then why did James and the other Nazoreans not provide Saul with more information?

One relevant factor may simply be that Jesus was not such an important figure for the Nazoreans as he became for the Christians. He had been, as described, a messianic contender for the throne of Israel. But others came after him, such as Theudas [Judas] and James and Simon (sons of this or an earlier Judas) who were either from other messianic lines or, possibly, rivals from the same messianic line (2). Either way, Jesus was superseded.

Even if he had survived crucifixion, he may subsequently have died by the time that Saul had become active and involved in creating a sect of his own. Coupled with this, Saul was not at the outset primarily or even at all concerned with Jesus.

What his letters and Acts show is that he was seeking to create a form of Judaism for gentiles, without the requirement for circumcision, many of the Jewish dietary requirements or indeed respect for the Mosaic Law as a whole.

This brought him into conflict with the Nazoreans who were not merely a movement within Judaism but its prime force in the circumstance of direct Roman rule. So James, as the religious leader representing Jews, could generate a letter to be sent to gentiles, who wished to be associated as 'god fearers' specifying what rules they should observe (Acts 15, 19-21). At a time when the Roman-appointed Sadducee high priest was seen by Jews as a Roman stooge and treated with scant respect, James according to early sources took on the role, even entering the holy of holies in the temple, on the day of atonement (3). He was in effect an opposition high priest, the representative of the Jewish people, a counter to the representatives for the Romans.

Saul persisted in advocating disregard for Jewish Law, even at the minimal level set out by James, among the communities of gentile followers he had begun to set up at Antioch in Syria and elsewhere.

When the final 'breakdown' came, graphically described in Acts 21, 20-36, it was about 20 years after the crucifixion and it was Jewish Law and not Jesus that was at issue.

Apart from the fact that Jesus, no longer a current messianic contender and quite likely dead, was not a central figure for Jews, there was actually little or no dialogue between the Jews or Nazorean Jews and what was to become a breakaway sect. This is because Saul avoided interaction with the Nazoreans over a very long period. Galatians even records a gap of 14 years between Saul's visits to Jerusalem. That covered most of the time that Saul and James and his followers were supposed to be cooperating.

There was thus for much of the time no contact at all. The two sides were in practice operating separately.

If Jesus were still alive, the Nazoreans would have continued to keep his whereabouts a secret out of regard for his safety. They might, moreover, have had especial reason to keep it all from Saul who appears to have been a minor member of the Herodian family. Since Saul was largely absent, and entirely absent for very many years, this should not have been at all difficult.

Saul claimed to have Roman citizenship by birth, something that was granted to the descendants of Herod for restoring Palestine to Roman rule. He moved in fairly exalted circles, on easy terms with Herodian kings and Roman governors.

He also had Herodian relatives, including Aristobulus and Herodion, or 'little Herod', (Romans 16, 10-11) who were in fact close relatives of his namesake Saulus who, in the pages of Josephus' *Antiquities* with his brother Costobarus plundered the property of 'those weaker than themselves'. There is a strong case that Saul/Paul in the New Testament was based on the same character Saulus that Josephus described.

Saul's aim, as described in Acts, was to take the Jew's

monotheistic religion to the diaspora, among gentiles, Jews and their associated gentile 'god fearers', who adhered to most of the Mosaic Law but were not full converts.

Saul made little headway among Jews, who were rightly suspicious of Saul's intentions and resentful of his attempts to wean away their god-fearer followers. But he began to have more success among gentiles.

Saul appears to have been aware of the story of Jesus, though not of the Jewish narrative that was ultimately used in generating the core of the gospel of Mark. He could even have used his dreams or visions of Jesus, a recently martyred Nazorean leader, as a means of claiming the right to go over the heads of the present leadership centred on James. Whatever they said, he could have claimed recourse to a higher authority, one hard to contradict since Jesus was (apparently) already deceased and only appearing personally to Saul in dreams (4).

Many of the new converts brought with them their existing pagan beliefs. I suggest that they began to incorporate these with stories in circulation about Jesus, most notably that no body was found when the tomb was opened and that there were subsequently reported sightings. It required no great leap of imagination for Jesus to be transformed into an amalgam of the myths of Mithras and Dionysus, as a dying and resurrecting god-man. Saul was probably well aware that this transformation had no justifiable basis, and indeed he reaffirmed his belief that Jesus was born 'according to the flesh' (Romans 1, 3). But he was unable to control the development of what were powerful and appealing ideas among his scattered communities of followers.

Saul's letters demonstrate a struggle to come to terms with this, in a progression by which Jesus gradually came to be regarded as a having a special relationship with God, by virtue of death and resurrection (5).

These developments would have taken time to establish. They had either not happened, or had not progressed to the point at which they would have come to the notice of Nazorean Jewish leaders in Jerusalem by the time of the climactic rift with Saul around CE 55. What certainly had come to the notice of James and the others were reports of Saul advocating that the Torah no longer needed to be observed, that circumcision was unnecessary and the Jewish dietary requirements should be abandoned. Summoned to Jerusalem, Saul was first admonished and then made to undergo the penance of a seven-day purification rite. There were four other men 'under a vow' and Saul was forced to pay for the expenses of having their heads shaved as well as his own.

The ostensible purpose of this was that 'all will know that there is nothing in what they have been told about you, but that you yourself observe and guard the Law' (Acts 21, 24).

Before the rite was completed, Saul was dragged from the temple and attacked by a crowd, apparently intent on beating him to death, but saved just in time by the intervention of Roman soldiers.

It seems that there may have been an element of intent, since those in the temple must have known what would happen to Saul once he stepped or was taken outside. He was told, in words that conveyed more than a hint of a threat, 'What then is to be [done]? The multitude must needs come together, for they will know that you have come' (Acts 21, 22, *Codex Sinaiticus*) (6).

Saul fortuitously survived and after this point there would have been a complete break between Jews, inside and outside of Palestine, and his new sect. As Acts had it, it was at Antioch that the gentile followers of Saul were first called 'Christians'.

The story that was taken up, in the sect's quest for information about its adopted central figure, may have surfaced or been in circulation after the destruction of the temple at the end of the uprising in CE 70. It was possibly a pesher-style analysis of the circumstances of Jesus' crucifixion and claimed survival, taking in the context of Jewish prophecies. The ending that was there provided form and coherence to the story, with John as Elijah (in spirit) heralding the coming of the last days, and with Jesus' reappearance as the last great sign, vindicating John.

The ending was, I have argued, taken back earlier into the text by an early Christian editor and adapted to become the story of the transfiguration.

This Jewish narrative, underlying Mark, told of the reappearance of Jesus before a crowd at Mount Hermon. As part of the drama that was yet to be recorded, these witnesses – that is, the people in the crowd – would not have had a narrative to help them in their interpretation of what was happening. They would have learned that Jesus had survived. That was what the Nazoreans said and that was what their written account would subsequently state.

But this account may have been no more intended as a public record than the analyses of psalm 37 and Habakkuk, against contemporary events, stored in caves at Qumran and only accidentally coming to light nearly nineteen centuries later. At some early point, the commentary that became Mark was acquired by followers of Saul and his evolving, breakaway sect. It was not, however, immediately available to Jews.

Jesus in the meantime had disappeared from public view and, as the years passed, some of the witnesses to the events on Mount Hermon may have begun to have doubts as to who it was they had seen. The story, in remembering and retelling, would have changed and taken on new elements. Jews were accustomed to their legendary heroes, like Elijah and Methusaleh, being taken directly up into heaven. That, in one of the accounts circulating, could have been the assumed explanation for Jesus' failure to reappear.

When Christians came later to try to provide a substitute for the ending that was by then missing from Mark, with its narrative developed from an appropriated Jewish text, they tapped into the oral testimony that had been passed on and down among Jews. This would explain some elements that are in the later gospels from around the end of the first century and the 12 verses that were added to Mark at some time in the early second century.

Failure to recognise Jesus or doubt/disbelief that the person seen was Jesus is a common theme (Matthew 28, 17; Luke 24, 11; 24, 16; 24, 41; John 20, 14; 20, 25; 21, 4). The added ending of Mark and Luke, in the early papyrus manuscript **p**75, both have Jesus taken up into heaven (Mark 16, 19; Luke 24, 51). So also does the gnostic gospel of Peter which has Jesus spiritually 'taken up', after his cry from the cross, and then physically rising up beyond the realm of the demiurge to a higher heaven, after being helped from the tomb.

The uncertainty and lack of substance that characterise the gospel post-crucifixion accounts are a reflection of their source. This was an oral tradition that developed in the absence of any evidence of Jesus beyond a few days or weeks, following the crucifixion.

So, there is a satisfactory, or at least plausible, explanation for a second phase in the development of a Christian narrative. But that still leaves the need to understand what happened in the first phase, when an ending to Mark was cut that can clearly be identified as once having been present.

The ending that I have identified as lying beneath the transfiguration narrative provides what is expected from the surviving part of Mark, a journey by Jesus to Galilee with those of his close supporters, who had not already accompanied him there, following on to meet him.

Such an account would, however, have presented some early Christians, seeking a passion narrative, with problems.

Saul in his writings offers no awareness of gospel accounts, so he was probably dead by the time these came to be written down and so unable to influence events. These accounts would therefore have begun to evolve, with the compilation of Mark, from about CE 70-80.

The Christian Jesus had been generated through the influence of pagan beliefs among the sect's new gentile converts. Jesus had been subsumed as a son of God, in parallel with the story of the god Zeus whose liaison with the mortal woman Semele, produced Dionysus who was thereby part divine. In several versions, Dionysus is killed but then miraculously brought back to life.

So the 'Christ' that came about was a semi-divine being, a son of God who could by divine power be made to live again.

That is what the early Christians expected. But that is not at all what they had in their newly discovered Jewish narrative. There were elements suggesting that Jesus had survived.

His return to life did not, in this appropriated story, come about through some, astonishing divine act. It was accomplished through the efforts of helpers. Then Jesus had to recuperate. Then he made a journey of around 80 miles, with three assistants, that took him several days.

He had a secret meeting with sympathisers. They discussed the prospect of his exile, in view of the certainty that the Romans, once the news got to them, would have sought to recapture him.

This was not the story of a divine being, who would not have needed to wait to recover, whose wounds could have been miraculously made to disappear and who, if that were required by the narrative, could be made to reappear instantly anywhere, including Galilee.

It was all too gritty and natural, not what was required for the Dionysus-style figure that pagan converts to Christianity had brought with them.

Furthermore, in the Jewish exposition or narrative and quite possibly a first Christian version based on it, Jesus played an ancillary role. His triumph (surviving and rising) over the ordeal of crucifixion served as both a last, great sign and as a confirmation of the validity of prophecy.

The central figure was in fact arguably John the Baptist. Just as Jesus, the 'suffering servant', had triumphed over adversity so John had taken on, actually or symbolically, the spirit of Elijah, returning again to herald the last days.

But the new Christians wanted their anointed one (messiah) to take on a more central and a more divine role. The coming of the last days, the kingdom of god 'with power' (Mark 9, 1) survives, I suggest, in the text as a relic of the more original ending provided by the underlying Jewish narrative. It is now qualified by a reference, introduced by Christian editing in the preceding verse, to the 'son of man' coming 'in the glory of his father with the holy angels' (Mark 8, 38).

What this verse says is that this is what the next verse (Mark 9, 1) is about, whatever might be thought to the contrary. To reinforce the point, two other subsequent statements attributed to Jesus have been placed in the text, with similar wording and intent. One is within the little apocalypse, at Mark 13, 26, when 'in those days' they 'will see the son of man coming in clouds with great power and glory'. Jesus is also given to respond, under questioning by the high priest that 'you will see the son of man seated at the right hand of the power and coming with the clouds of heaven' (Mark 14, 62).

These are, just like Jesus' given predictions of his death and resurrection discussed earlier (p 44), formulaic Christian interjections, this time predicting with reference to Daniel 7, 13 ('with the clouds of heaven there came one like a son of man') Jesus' future return to earth.

So, instead of just God coming in the last days, the early Christians made it Jesus with God coming in the last days.

This did not square with the underlying Jewish text which had Jesus as a sign of the imminent end times and as God's suffering servant, restored from the brink of death. Not only that, but Jesus in the underlying Jewish account had walked or ridden on the back of a mule from Jerusalem to Galilee.

The Christian perception was by contrast of a spirit Jesus who was going to make a miraculous comeback. So, in fashioning or refashioning Mark, this was a reason why this part of the text was cut, amended and moved back to an earlier point where it could be fitted in to the narrative.

This left Mark with an inconclusive and unsatisfactory ending, which proved hard to remedy, if only because almost anything that could be made logically to follow on would have conflicted with the newly developed Christian theology.

In some ways, this did not matter much, since other gospels came to be written and proved more popular, most especially Matthew which was in effect a complete rewrite of Mark. Although what the author of Matthew put in is vague, at least it can be said that this gospel has an ending that completes the narrative.

That the very early Christians had a framework into which the Jewish text could be slotted, after being suitably amended, is indicated by Saul's letters to the Thessalonians. The first of these dealt with concerns over what will happen to those who were already dead in the last days, whether they might be left out from being gathered up into heaven. Saul provides the reassurance that 'the dead in Christ will rise first; then we the living who remain shall be caught up in the clouds together with them to meet the Lord in the air' (1 Thessalonians 4, 17).

The reference to clouds is again suggestive of the prophecy of Daniel, though it is not clear whether the 'Lord' in the air refers to the 'Lord Jesus' or the 'Lord God' or maybe both (7). It has to be said that this letter shows signs of being overwritten with some doctrinal references to Jesus (8).

While Jews recognised 'No Lord but God', Christians have also applied the appellation 'Lord' to Jesus. This has had the effect of promoting both the standing of Jesus and also the doctrine of the identification of Jesus with God.

Just as Jesus' foreknowledge of his fate and return (second

coming) is projected into the narrative that formed Mark, so in Acts, Simon (Peter) is given to argue that the disciples 'speaking in other tongues' was a fulfilment of Joel's prophecy concerning the last days when God would 'pour out' his spirit upon all flesh (Acts 2, 14-17).

The Jewish perspective was that God would come to redeem Israel, restore a kingdom of heaven on earth and/or deliver a last judgment, whereas here in Acts, the probably early second-century author has interjected a resurrected and exalted Jesus pouring out the manifestation of speaking in tongues to the disciples, as a sign of the last days (Acts 2, 33).

This contains just a trace of what some zealous Jews may have believed in the mid-first century, following the crucifixion, according to the interwoven prophetic analysis that underlay Mark. Jesus' near miraculous recovery was the final sign of the imminent end times. But these Nazoreans, keepers of the covenant, went on being observant Jews, attending the temple and their local synagogues, keeping the Law. For the first few years, there were no Christians and no second coming of Jesus expected by Jews.

Saul, I suggest, had used the character Jesus, whom he claimed was appearing to him in dreams, as a means of seeking to circumvent the authority of the Nazorean Jews who were, at a time of direct Roman rule, the zealous and popular heart of Judaism. Saul's aim was to take the monotheistic message of Judaism to gentiles, in a simpler and more direct form, shorn of the weight of detailed Jewish laws, dietary restrictions and the requirement for circumcision.

His first pagan converts brought with them beliefs and rituals, centred on a dying and resurrecting god-man, into which Jesus was incorporated. Saul had to struggle to reconcile his position with developments among his scattered churches, which were not entirely within his control.

After Saul's death, there was interest from both sides in this debate in finding more about Jesus. The outcome was an account, attributed to Mark or John Mark, which probably married oral testimony with a written pesher-style analysis of the misfortunes of Nazorean zealots. This account had the ending of Mark that was turned into the transfiguration story.

As appropriated, this early Mark was no longer Jewish testimony but neither did it reflect all the doctrine, including the divinity of Jesus, which has subsequently been projected into the story.

The theme of a resurrected Jesus was powerful and appealing and that is why the ending that did not entirely fit was cut, modified and reabsorbed into the main body of the text.

The early Christians, at the same time, displaced Jesus as a sign of the end times into the position of being part of the end times. When the ending of the Jewish narrative that became Mark was folded back, that is how it was adapted and reinforced with statements attributed to Jesus, foretelling his own second coming.

It was expected to happen soon, as is indicated in both 1 and 2 Thessalonians, written maybe no more than twenty years after the crucifixion. But, as the years passed, the argument became harder to sustain.

By the mid-second century, there was a gathering crisis of belief. As I have argued, p 75, part of the purpose of 2 Peter was to rally the faithful, by providing testimony that supported the idea that Jesus would still one day return. The author of this pseudepigraph dealt with the crisis by adducing Simon Peter himself, as an authority who had supposedly witnessed Jesus' 'majesty', in the transfiguration story and also be extending the time frame. Thus, for the Lord, 'a thousand years are like one day'.

In spite of the very clear indications from words that are later Christian interpolations, put into the mouth of a long-dead Jewish messiah, there are many people nineteen centuries later who both believe in a second coming and that Jesus himself had predicted it.

One of the lessons of history is that ideas that that are compelling, that cater to very basic needs, are likely to survive, regardless of evidence.

Wherever Jesus was, if ever Jesus was, James and his fellow Nazoreans were the ones who knew. But they had no voice and they lost much of their following after the disaster that was, for many thousands of Jews (for each of them personally) the end of time.

This was when the uprising was crushed and their temple destroyed.

It was indeed the end for one great movement and a style of worship in Judaism. For the sect that broke way, it provided an opportunity and a beginning.

Conclusion

My concern in analysing the text has been to look for its origins, functions and intentions. This is a logical exercise that could be and is often applied to other forms of literature, including the religious myths of other cultures. What makes the Christian stories particularly intriguing is that many prove, on examination, to have had Jewish origins and can be traced to a time and a context, when a new sect split away amidst considerable acrimony and conflict. The need that Christians had to retain their Jewish pedigree for links back to Jesus, while distancing themselves from Jesus' Jewish roots, created interesting tensions that sometimes show up in the text.

The transfiguration story, like others in gospels and other parts of the New Testament, proves on examination to have an underlying Jewish narrative, edited and adapted long ago by early Christian writers.

My analysis indicates that it has two other, unique and remarkable characteristics. It was moved, as a substantial and possibly almost entire passage, from another part of the text. It had provided, in its essentials, the climax to Mark, the original and prime source for the other gospels. It is, reordered and much mutilated, the ending of Mark that is now missing and had been thought lost.

This is what I consider to be the best available interpretation, on the basis of all the evidence, one which incidentally drastically reduces the number of otherwise inexplicable and discordant elements.

My conclusion breaks the deadlock between two great divisions that have been reached in textual analysis of the transfiguration. These are firstly between those who see it as entirely allegorical and those who see it as relating to some real event. It will be noted that, while there are grounds for arguing that the story may be fictional and as such would serve as allegory, my analysis of the evidence provides qualified support for the position that there is an historical basis (see p 108). There is a real, underlying Jewish narrative and a strong possibility that this in turn relates to some real events. But these are not the events that Christian commentators bring with them, as a preconceived set of beliefs, to their studies of the text.

The early writer who examined the outcome of a misadventure, against prior prophecy, was seeking to understand it as part of God's plan for the Jewish people. He was seeking to explain, or he was arguing for, or both, the survival of a messianic leader whose mission had failed. For Jews now and then, there was no resurrection.

As it can now be reconstructed, the early narrative expressed hope for the future liberation of Jews and a reward for the righteous in heaven. It sought to retrieve something positive from what had been a calamitous, misjudged confrontation.

This was, however, soon to be overshadowed and overwhelmed by an even greater disaster, the failure of the first Jewish uprising.

After this, even their original story was taken from them.

The second major division lies between those who have argued that the transfiguration sequence originated as a post-resurrection story, which Mark then appropriated to use within his narrative, as against others who maintain that it is correctly located within the lifetime of Jesus.

The argument that the transfiguration may be a misplaced resurrection account appears to have begun around the beginning of the twentieth century with Bacon (*The Transfiguration Story; A Study of the Problem of the Sources of Our Synoptic Gospels*) and has since been taken up by others, including Carlston (*Transfiguration and Resurrection*).

My analysis indicates strongly that it was relocated from some other point by the early author or editor of Mark. However, the event to which the transfiguration relates is not post-resurrection but *post-crucifixion*, and as such it forms part of the continuation of the narrative.

This distinction is absolutely crucial and explains many of the difficulties that have been encountered in the debate.

For example, Stein (*Is the Transfiguration (Mark 9, 2-8) a Misplaced Resurrection Account?*) has argued, on a number of grounds, against those who maintain that the transfiguration story is a post-resurrection account. His case includes the 'form critical' arguments initially put forward by Dodd (*The Appearances of the Risen Christ: an Essay in Form Criticism of the Gospels*) that distinguish it from post-resurrection stories in the gospels.

In these stories, Jesus 'appears' to one or more of his family and followers and speaks to them. He is always alone, there is no voice from heaven and his clothes do not shine. But, in the transfiguration narrative, he is already there with three of his disciples and remains with them. It is Moses and Elijah, not Jesus, that 'appear' and just as suddenly disappear. Jesus' clothes become radiant and the voice of God is heard from a cloud. On the basis of these several differences of form, it is argued that the transfiguration cannot have originated in the same way and be the same kind of material as the stories of appearances, following the crucifixion, that are in all of the gospels (except the more original, shorter version of Mark whose ending is cut).

This is, of course, entirely correct. But the objections raised by Dodd and Stein lose their force, once it is recognised that the transfiguration account is not in any case one of the recollections that have been passed on in retelling, eventually to be written down and used by gospel writers seeking to make good the absence of an ending to Mark. It is instead a continuation of the narrative, though of course much adapted in being reused and relocated in the text. It is therefore no surprise then that it reads as part of this narrative, rather than as one of the fragmentary, supernatural oral tales that have been used to augment the later gospels.

So it can be agreed that the voice from a cloud was added, as were the names of Moses and Elijah applied to the people that Jesus and his companions met. The shining of face or clothes may also have been an elaboration, or were there originally as a circumstantial detail, to be expected from an encounter on a high mountain where there was snow.

But Jesus in the story goes to the mountain with his three companions, because that is what is being described in the underlying narrative as having happened, after Jesus had survived and been revived, following the crucifixion. Because he is already there, he does not need to 'appear' to talk to his companions. He is indeed reported as talking to them on the way back down the mountain and then subsequently to the crowd waiting to see him.

Other commentators have had problems, perhaps in part because of their preconceptions but also because they have not looked at the text carefully enough.

The restriction of considering the transfiguration text limited to Mark 9, 2-8, or Mark 9, 2-10 is clearly misconceived. Heil, for example (*The Transfiguration of Jesus: Narrative Meaning and Function of Mark 9, 2-8, Matthew 17, 1-8 and Luke 9, 28-36*), deliberately limited his analysis to the text up to the point where the two other men at the meeting have left. He has thereby missed the significance of the (now dispersed) conversation with the scribes and the reaction of the crowd. He has failed to understand the significance of the crucial pronouncement attributed to Jesus, concerning John the Baptist and Elijah, which I have suggested forms part of the culmination of Mark. He has also been unable to spot the dislocation that defines the end of the transfiguration sequence, having left it out of his consideration.

The story has a beginning, when the four ascend the mountain, a middle part that describes what happened there and an end that describes what happened on the way back down and when they meet the other disciples, the crowd and the disbelieving scribes.

Whether or not some scribes were actually present at such an historical event, post the crucifixion, the reason that they are there in the story is to provide a foil for the argument over the return of Elijah.

It was believed that the last days could not happen until Elijah had returned. The argument in the underlying narrative of Mark, put succinctly, is that Elijah did return as John the Baptist, at least in spirit. Jesus' remarkable survival, as the suffering servant, confirms the power of prophecy and is of itself a sign. So, also it can be believed that Elijah had come.

The story of the transfiguration is in form a coherent whole and it is at the beginning and end of this coherent whole that there are dislocations defining the passage as a whole, from 9, 2 to 9, 16 (plus maybe 9, 1), as having been relocated from somewhere else.

That somewhere else was, on the simplest and best interpretation, the early version of Mark or the underlying Jewish narrative from which the Christian compiler was working.

The very early editor (or editors) of Mark did not just move the text from one position to another. He reworked some details, so as to give them a supernatural slant. He added elements to support Christian doctrine and cut out others that conflicted with this, including the discussion of what Jesus should do next.

He rearranged the text internally to disguise what was the topic of conversation with the scribes.

What I suggest may have been the crucial culmination of Mark, which has Jesus as the physical sign that all was accomplished in order for the 'last days' to happen, was moved back within the story and qualified.

In this way, much of the Jewish text was preserved, while being made to serve another purpose. The word so retained could be regarded as still sacred, the word of God mediated by divine inspiration as the Christian word.

Surprisingly, in seeking to understand the transfiguration, another great mystery may have been resolved.

The ending of Mark that was thought to be lost has, in plain view, been there all the time.

References

Allison D C, *Elijah must come first*, JBL vol 3, no 2, 1984, pp 256-258.

Atwill J & Braunheim S, *Redating the radiocarbon dating of the Dead Sea Scrolls*, Dead Sea Discoveries, vol 11, no 2, 2004

Bacon B W, *The Transfiguration Story; A Study of the Problem of the Sources of Our Synoptic Gospels*, AJT, vol 6, no 2, 1902, pp 236-265

Baigent M & Leigh R, *The Dead Sea Scrolls Deception*, Arrow Books, 2006,

Black D A (ed), *Perspectives on the Ending of Mark*, Broadman & Holman, 2008

British Library, National Library of Russia, St Catherine's Monastery, Leipzig University Library, *Codex Sinaiticus*, published online 2009

Canart P, Bogaert P M & Pisano S (contributors), *Bibliorum Sacrorum Graecorum Codex Vaticanus B*, vol I facsimile text, vol 2 Prolegomena: essays and index, Istituto Poligrafico e Zecca delo Strato, 1999

Comfort P W & Barrett D P, *The Text of the Earliest New Testament Greek Manuscripts*, Tyndale House, 2001

Carlston C E, *Transfiguration and Resurrection*, JBL, vol 1, no 80, Sept 1961, pp 233-240

Cresswell P A, *Jesus the terrorist*, O Books, 2010

Cresswell P A, *The Invention of Jesus*, Watkins, 2013

Cresswell P A, *The Women who went to the Tomb*, The Heretic, vol 3, 2013

Cresswell P A, *How the Church Changed its Texts*, Ethical Record, The Proceedings of the Conway Hall Ethical Society, vol 119, no 3, March 2014, pp 3-9

Crossan J D, *The Historical Jesus*, T & T Clark, Edinburgh, 1991

Dodd C H, *The Appearances of the Risen Christ: an Essay in Form*

Criticism of the Gospels. in Nineham D E, *Studies in the Gospels,* Wiley-Blackwell, 1955

Eisenman R, *Paul as Herodian,* Institute for Jewish-Christian Origins, 1996

Eisenman R, *The Dead Sea Scrolls and the First Christians,* Element Books, 1996

Eisenman R, *James, the Brother of Jesus,* Faber and Faber, 1997

Eisenman R, *The New Testament Code,* Watkins, 2006

Eisenman R & Wise M, *The Dead Sea Scrolls Uncovered,* Element Books, 1992

Faierstein M M, *Why do the scribes say that Elijah must come first?,* JBL, vol 100, no 1, 1981, pp 75-86.

Farmer W R, *The last twelve verses of Mark,* Cambridge University Press, 2005

Feldman L H (trans), *Jewish Antiquities,* Books 18-19, Harvard University Press, 1965

Feldman L H (trans), *Jewish Antiquities,* Book 20, Harvard University Press, 1965

Fitzmyer J A, *More about Elijah coming first,* JBL, vol 104, no 2, pp 295-296

Heil J P, *The Transfiguration of Jesus: Narrative Meaning and Function of Mark 9, 2-8, Matthew 17, 1-8 and Luke 9, 28-36,* Analecta Biblica 144, Gregorian and Biblical Press 2000

Maccoby H, *The Myth Maker,* Weidenfeld & Nicholson, 1986

Lee S S, *Jesus' Transfiguration and the Believer's Transformation,* Mohr Siebeck, 2009

Metzger B M, *Manuscripts of the Greek Bible: an Introduction to Palaeography,* Oxford University Press 1981

Metzger B M, *The Text of the New Testament: its Transmission, Corruption and Restoration,* Oxford University Press, 1992

Moses A D A, *Matthew's Transfiguration and the Jewish-Christian Controversy,* Sheffield Academic Press, 1996

Reid B, *The transfiguration: A Source and Redactive-Critical Study of Luke 9, 28-36,* Gabalda 1993

Roberts A & Donaldson J, *The Ante-Nicene Fathers*, Eerdmans, 1995 (for *Pseudoclementine Recognitions* and *Homilies*)

Silberman N A, *The Hidden Scrolls*, BCA, 1995

Stein R H, *Is the Transfiguration (Mark 9, 2-8) a Misplaced Resurrection Account?* JBL, vol 95, no 1, March 1976 pp 79-96

Vermes G, *The Dead Sea Scrolls in English*, Penguin Books, 1962

Williamson GA, (trans), *The Jewish War*, Penguin Books, 1981

Notes

Preface

1 The semantic range for a particular word or possible lack of an exact equivalence may generate a situation of choice in translation.

2 Some theologically motivated interpretations will be encountered in the course of analysis. A classic example is provided by the mis-rendering of 'Nazarene' or 'Nazorean' as meaning 'from Nazareth'. See chapter 8, 'Nazarene or Nazareth', of *The Invention of Jesus*.

Another case is provide by Luke 23, 32 where 'two other criminals were also led away with him to be executed' is usually translated, less convincingly, as 'two others also, who were criminals, were led away to be executed with him'.

3 See pp 272-276 of *Jesus the terrorist*.

4 Saul's remarks indicate that he was sensitive to criticisms that he was living off others (1 Corinthians 9 3-7), while asserting his right to 'reap' material benefits from his followers (ibid, verse 11). He was collecting money, ostensibly for the 'saints' in Jerusalem, but it must be wondered how much, given the hostility and ultimate breakdown between the Nazoreans and Saul, ever got to them. The Roman Governor Felix is described as cultivating Saul over a long period, in the hope of getting money from him (Acts 24, 26).

There are oblique tales in *Antiquities* and the *Acts of Peter* that could be taken as suggesting that Saul/Paul was stealing from others.

For a more detailed analysis of Saul's role, see chapter 5 of *Jesus the terrorist*.

5 See chapter 8 of *The Invention of Jesus*.

6 See chapter 3, pp 73-79 of *Jesus the terrorist.*

7 This is discussed further on pp 81-82 of *Jesus the terrorist* and extensively in *James the brother of Jesus* by Robert Eisenman.

8 See *Jesus the terrorist* pp 140-141. There is a useful summary chart of the Herodian family tree in Appendix IV of this book, pp 420-421, which, in conjunction with the analysis on p 148, indicates how closely related Saul was to Aristobulus and 'little Herod'.

9 See *The Invention of Jesus*, p 208

10 See *The Invention of Jesus* pp 172-174

11 I am not here concerned with the exegesis of scripture, construction of conceptual frameworks or elaboration of doctrine, as for example in works (see *References)* by A D A Moses and Simon S Lee, except in so far as a study is relevant to the critical examination of a text.

Introduction

1 See chapter 7, 'The primacy of Mark', of *The Invention of Jesus.*

2 Two examples are described here in chapter six, pp 83-88. There is also an analysis of other stories in chapter 11, 'Myth and Method', of *Jesus the terrorist.*

Chapter 1

1 This is dealt with further in examining the text. See p 42 and p 66 of chapter 4.

Chapter 2

1 For discussion of different aspects of the significance of this, see *Jesus the terrorist*, pp 27-31, and *The Invention of Jesus*, pp 269-70.

Chapter 4

1 See chapter 11 of *The Invention of Jesus.*

2 Barbara Reid makes the case, in *The transfiguration: A Source*

and Redactive-Critical Study of Luke 9, 28-36, that the author of Luke had an older and more primary source which he supplemented with the narrative from Mark. This, however, contradicts very strong evidence that Mark was the primary source for both Matthew and Luke (see chapter 7 of *The Invention of Jesus*.)

Some changes were made to Mark, subsequent to the creation of both Matthew and Luke. This, for example, accounts for the description of Jesus being from Nazareth, later interpolated at Mark 1, 9 and so not present in the copy made by the author of Matthew (see pp 154-161 of *The Invention of Jesus*).

I agree that probably early Mark or more certainly the Jewish narrative source for Mark had 'two men' and that the names Moses and Elijah were later introduced into all the synoptics.

It may also be that early Mark or the Jewish narrative source for Mark had the reference to EXOΔON and, while this was later cut from Mark, it survived in the copy made in generating Luke.

3 See note 2 to Preface.

4 Eusebius quotes two extracts from a now lost work by Papias (approx CE 70-163), which indicate how at an early stage it was perceived the gospels of Mark and Matthew were compiled. According to Papias, using as source John the Elder, 'Mark' simply wrote down what Simon Peter had told him, but not in an ordered form. The second extract indicated that Matthew 'arranged' the logia [things said or done] in an ordered fashion.

The perception was that the early gospel writers worked from material that was not necessarily in any good or correct order, and so put it together as they saw fit.

5 The drawback to other analyses that treat different portions of the text as the transfiguration narrative is that these

explain less, have obvious deficiencies and are less coherent. So, for example Bacon (*The Transfiguration Story; A Study of the Problem of the Sources of Our Synoptic Gospels*) and others since have treated Mark 9, 2-10 as interpolated. However, Jesus came down the mountain with his three, key companions and then reached the [rest of the] disciples who had gone on (as foreshadowed) to meet up with him in Galilee. So Mark 9, 14-16 has to be part of the transfiguration sequence, and not the surrounding text, and so also must be Mark 9, 11-13 though, as I have argued, it is slightly displaced.

6 There is a case that at least one version of an ending of Mark, possibly nearer to the underlying Jewish source for the passion sequence, may have survived for much longer, either neglected or forgotten. I have provided evidence that an ending of Mark was suppressed in creating Codex Sinaiticus. See chapter 11, 'The lost ending of Mark' and subsequent chapters of *The Invention of Jesus.*

7 See chapter 2 and pp 306-308 of *Jesus the terrorist.*

8 See pp 388-393 of *Jesus the terrorist.*

9 Lazarus, brother of Mary and Martha in the gospel of John, was arguably related to Jesus as his brother-in-law. In the synoptic gospels, this same character may have undergone a transformation as the 'daughter' of Jairus, restored to life by Jesus. In the *Jewish War,* Eleazar [Lazarus] appears as the zealot captain, son of Jairus, who held Masada and led a mass suicide in the face of certain defeat by the Romans. See pp 307-309 of *Jesus the terrorist.*

10 Simon Peter is made to appear vacillating over the question of Jewish dietary restriction, Galatians 3, 11-12 and Acts 11, 1-10. This may be as much a projection as his supposed weakness in denying being a follower of Jesus.

Chapter 5

1 Retrojecting into a narrative predictions of events that had already happened, at the time of writing, is not an uncommon literary device. So, for example, the author of the book of Daniel, has Daniel predicting to King Nebuchadnezzar the rising of four kingdoms before God sets up his own, everlasting heavenly kingdom. However, the author was writing in the second century BC, when all the events had taken place, apart from the final divine intervention. See *Censored Messiah*, pp 67-70.

Chapter 6

1 If it is conceived, as Christian editors might have, that Jesus had become a spirit being who could dematerialise and reappear at will, then there would of course have been no problem with his going on to Galilee after the crucifixion on his own.

2 See pp 358-360 of *Jesus the terrorist*.

3 A large marriage feast would have necessitated substantial vessels to contain wine and the purification jars could have served such a purpose. Residue of the original wine might thus have been there already or could have been added incidentally from the skins used to fill the jars with water. Either way, what Jesus may have made, in the story, was water flavoured with a hint of wine, a refreshing change for guests who may already have drunk quite a lot.

4 Given that there are reports that James and Simon/Simeon remained celibate, it may be that the inner council of the Nazoreans remained celibate, as did that of the similar (or possibly, identical group, the Essenes). But Jesus, as the eldest of several brothers, and thus the chief messianic contender, would have had an obligation to marry and if possible provide male heirs. There is no record of any that survived.

5 It is similarly not possible to 'prove' that Jesus was married to the person who turns up in the text as his constant companion, behaving on many occasions just as a Jewish wife would, that is Mary/Mary Magdalene, though this also is the most likely explanation. See *Jesus the terrorist*, pp 174-176.

6 See chapter 11 of *Jesus the terrorist*.

7 See pp 73-79 of *Jesus the terrorist*.

8 See for example, chapter 8, 'Gospel truth', of *Jesus the terrorist*, chapter 10, 'Women at the cross', of *The Invention of Jesus* and *The Women who Went to the Tomb*.

Chapter 7

1 There is an addition to Matthew verse 27, 49 in Codex Sinaiticus, followed by Codex Vaticanus, 'but another took his spear and pierced his side and out came water and blood'. While there are now no surviving earlier manuscripts for this part of Matthew, later copyists, who would have had such evidence available, do not include the additional material. This indicates quite strongly that the addition to the verse originated as an attempted harmonisation with John 19, 34 and was subsequently recognised, and discounted, as such. The added text also fits in uneasily, given that 'the others' have already said, 'Wait, let us see whether Elijah will come to save him.'

2 The Hebrew pesher was a form of commentary in which a writer used past prophecies in an effort to understand contemporary events. The Commentary on Habbakuk and the Commentary on Psalm 37, from among the Dead Sea Scrolls, provide good examples of this kind of text.

Dominic Crossan has argued, in *The Historical Jesus*, that the passion sequence in a more original 'Cross gospel', on which he believed the gospels of Peter and Mark were based, may have originated entirely as an interwoven pesher, created from a variety of Old Testament sources. It is my contention, in view of the number of basic elements in the narrative that have no apparent origin in prophecy, that there is an underlying Jewish story to which biblical prophecies were then related. See *Jesus the terrorist* pp 203-206.

Thus, the more original Jewish story, on which Mark was based, may have been created in pesher form, quite possibly in view of the number of allusions that there are in the text as a commentary on Isaiah.

It was not, however, just generated from this as a plausible story but better to understand and explain what had happened during and after an aborted uprising. It was fashioned to vindicate belief in the ultimate triumph of the righteous (see following chapters).

Chapter 8

1 For further detail, see pp 272-276 of *Jesus the terrorist.*

2 See pp 361-364 of *Jesus the terrorist.*

3 There is in Codex Sinaiticus Mark a change in style at the beginning of the transfiguration sequence, whereby new paragraphs are delineated by much greater degree of intrusion of the first character into the adjacent column margin.

This suggests that the scribe could at this point have switched from an exemplar that did not have this sequence to a different exemplar that had. It also implies, intriguingly, that the exemplar used up to that point may, correspondingly, have had in place some part of the ending of Mark after verse 16, 8.

Since a version of Mark with such an ending was evidently not available to the authors of Matthew and Luke, it would thus appear that the scribe had access to a version of Mark surviving from a very early period.

I have argued in *The Invention of Jesus* that the introduction a second scribe to produce three single sheets was with the aim of making crucial changes to the text. One of these sheets, covering the last part of Mark and the beginning of Luke, shows signs of both major compression and stretching of text, which may be to do with decision changes over what to include in the last part of Mark.

See chapters 8 and following of *The Invention of Jesus.*

Codex Sinaiticus is an important manuscript from a period when the Church was disseminating its message under the auspices of the Roman Empire and was, I have suggested, generated as an 'authorised' master copy.

4 See note 5 to chapter 4.

5 There is perhaps also an allusion here to Exodus 23, 20, in which God is given to promise to send the people of Israel an angel [messenger] to guard them on their journey back to the promised land.

6 The beginning of the War Scroll QMI, from the caves at Qumran, outlines the forthcoming attack by 'the sons of light against the forces of the sons of darkness'. As a result 'the dominion of the kittim [likely, Romans] shall come to an end', 'the sons of righteousness shall shine over all the ends of the earth, and 'at the time appointed by God his great excellence shall shine eternally'.

7 The commentaries on Habakkuk and psalm 37 describe the violence of the kittim (Romans), and a struggle involving three characters, 'the Wicked Priest' who amassed riches and plotted against the 'teacher of righteousness' and the 'liar' or 'spouter of lies' who 'led many astray', 'raised a congregation on deceit' and 'flouted the Law'. See pp 179-202 and pp 291-294 of *Jesus the terrorist*. Ananias, James and Saul/Paul provide a good fit for these characters and the time frame is feasible from palaeographic and radio carbon dating analysis.

Chapter 9

1 References, given almost in passing, include 1 Corinthians 1, 23; 1 Corinthians 2, 2; Galatians 3, 1; 2 Corinthians 13, 4.

2 See pp 299-323 of *Jesus the terrorist*.

3 Eusebius quotes Hegesippus, writing in the second century, as saying that James 'alone was allowed to enter the place of holiness'.

4 It was nevertheless resented and contradicted by the Ebionite followers of James. In a passage in the *PseudoClementine Homilies*, Simon Peter is given to challenge 'Simon Magus', apparently a stand-in for Saul, 'But can any one be rendered fit for instruction through apparitions?', adding 'And how did he appear to you, when you entertain opinions contrary to his teaching?'

5 See pp 171-174 of *The Invention of Jesus*.

6 Acts makes an effort to provide continuity and reconcile the conflict between the Nazoreans under James and Saul and his followers. This was essential if the newly founded Christian movement was to have a perceived unbroken 'apostolic' link back to Jesus, who was a Nazorean Jew. How difficult an exercise this was can be seen in the passage in which James and the 'elders' delivered judgement on Saul (Acts 21, 17-25).

While I have followed the line that Saul was at least superficially linked to the Nazoreans to start with, and then there was a break, another interpretation is that he never really was one of them.

Roman writ did not run to daily affairs, especially when it concerned disputes among what they might have perceived as troublesome, 'zealous' Jews. The Nazoreans did not have, or prudently did not seek to exercise, the same sort of power over Saul (as a minor member of the Herodian family) as they did over Ananias and Sapphira (Acts 5, 1-11). While Saul was not put to death for teaching against the

Law, it would, however, seem that he was allowed to be put in harm's way (Acts 21, 26-30).

7 While Jews recognised 'No Lord but God', Christians have also applied the appellation 'Lord' to Jesus. This has had the effects of promoting both the standing of Jesus and the doctrine of the identification of Jesus with God.

8 The first part of 1 Thessalonians, 1, 10, reads as more original but the ending of this verse 'and to wait for his son from heaven, whom he raised from the dead, Jesus who delivers us from the wrath to come' fits awkwardly and may thus be a later interpolation.